# 仁心孝德

孙衍庆

大医本色

科学出版社

北京

图书在版式编目（CIP）数据

仁心厚德　大医本色--孙衍庆/伍冀湘，张兆光主编，-北京：
　科学出版社，2010.6
ISBN 978-7-03-027704-6

Ⅰ．①仁　　Ⅱ．①伍...　　②张...　　①孙衍庆－生平事迹－画册
　Ⅳ．①K826.2-64

中国版本图书馆CIP数据核字（2010）第094239号

责任编辑：张颖兵　　吉正霞/责任校对：梅　莹
责任印刷：彭　超/封面设计：清华工美·青蓝广告

科　学　出　版　社 出版

北京东黄城根北街16号
邮政编码：100717
http://www.sciencep.com

版面设计：清华工美·青蓝广告
http://www.cyan-ad.com

武汉中远印务有限公司印刷
科学出版社发行　　各地新华书店经销
2010年4月第　一　版　　开本：787×1092　1/12
2010年4月第一次印刷　　印张：16
印数：1-3 000　　　　　字数：194 000
定价：180.00元
（如有印装质量问题，我社负责调换）

主　　编　　伍冀湘　张兆光

副 主 编　　程　军　白树功　罗　毅　周生来

编　　委　　房　琳　吴兴海　卢晓娣　王春媛

　　　　　　高世倩　刘凯燕

# 孙衍庆教授简介

　　孙衍庆现任北京安贞医院名誉院长，北京市心肺血管疾病高科技研究室首席专家，中华胸心血管外科学会名誉主任委员，北京生物工程学会名誉理事长，首都医科大学胸心血管外科教授，主任医师，硕士、博士及博士后教育流动站导师，北京大学医学部临床医学院客座教授。

　　孙衍庆教授生于1923年；1949年毕业于北京大学医学院（六年制），获学士学位；曾先后在北大医院、北京第三医院、北京友谊医院从事临床外科工作，历任友谊医院外科副主任、主任、实验外科主任、外科教研组主任和副院长；1979-1980年在阿根廷和美国波士顿医学院及休斯敦德克萨斯心脏中心访问学习考察，获得阿根廷医学通讯院士称号；1983-1987年任北京市卫生局局长兼党组书记，以后历任北京安贞医院院长兼北京市心肺疾病研究治疗中心主任，全国心血管疾病防治研究领导小组委员，国家医药卫生发明奖和进步奖评审委员会委员、副主任委员，北京科技协会常委、名誉委员，中华胸心血管外科杂志副总编、总编、名誉总编，北京生物医学工程学会理事长，北京生物工程杂志总编、名誉总编。是中国人民政治协商会议第七、第八届全国委员会委员；是第一批获得国家有突出贡献的专家；曾获"全国文教卫生系统先进工作者"、"全国百名好医生"等荣誉称号。

　　孙衍庆教授从医50多年，有丰富的实践经验和广博学识，集中攻克胸心血管外科的疑难病症。在国内首例进行了主动脉夹层动脉瘤根治手术（1982.4）、马凡综合征主动脉根部瘤根治手术（Bentall手术1985.3）、布加综合征经后腹腔右心房下腔静脉转流术等新手术，国内均已推广。创建限制性门腔静脉侧侧分流术治疗门静脉高压症，并形成一种重要的外科治疗方法。对瓣膜病伴发慢性房颤、离体供心保护、先心病、瓣膜病和人工生物瓣膜等多方面进行了深入研究，开拓了新手术领域。共发表论文205篇、著作7部，主编《现代胸心外科学》、《现代手术并发症学》、《门静脉高压症治疗研究》及高级医学教育《外科学》教材等。获得3项国家科技进步二等奖、19项省部级奖。为我国大动脉外科的发展做出了突出的贡献。

　　孙衍庆教授有高超的医术和高尚的医德，以及执著的敬业精神。他年逾八旬仍在辛勤工作，出专家门诊、指导疑难手术、伏案审稿编书，参加学术交流，关心医学科学前沿发展，在胸心外科领域默默耕耘。

# Profile of Professor Sun Yanqing

Sun Yanqing is currently the honorary president of Beijing Anzhen Hospital, chief expert at Beijing High-tech Center of Cardio-pulmonary Vessel Diseases, the honorary chairman of China Society of Thoracic and Cardiovascular Surgery, the honorary president of the council of Beijing Bioengineering Society, professor and chief physician at the Thoracic and Cardiovascular Surgery Department of Capital University of Medical Sciences, supervisor of doctoral candidates and centers for post-doctoral studies, and guest professor at the Clinical College of the Faculty of Medical Sciences of Beijing University.

He was born in 1923 and graduated from the Medical College (six years) of Beijing University with a bachelor's degree in 1949. He engaged in clinical surgery in Beijing University Hospital, the Third Hospital of Beijing, and Beijing Friendship Hospital, and was successively the vice director and director of the surgical department, director of experimental surgery, director of the Teaching and Research Group of Surgery, and vice president of Friendship Hospital. From 1979 to 1980, he visited and studied in Argentina, the Medical College in Boston, and Texas Heart Center in Houston, and received the Argentinean title of Corresponding Academician of Medical Sciences. From 1983 to 1987, he was chief and party secretary of Beijing Public Health Bureau. After that period, he was successively president of Beijing Anzhen Hospital and director of Beijing Center for the Research and Treatment of Cardio-pulmonary Diseases, a member of the National Leading Group for the Prevention, Treatment and Study of Cardiovascular Diseases, a member and vice chairman of the evaluation committee for National Invention Award and Progress Award for Medicine and Health Care, an executive member and honorary member of Beijing Science and Technology Association, deputy editor-in-chief, editor-in-chief and honorary editor-in-chief of China Thoracic and Cardiovascular Journal, director-general of Beijing Bioengineering Society, editor-in-chief and honorary editor-in-chief of Beijing Bioengineering Journal, and a member of the 7th and 8th National Committee of the CPPCC. He was one of the first to be designated as an 'expert with prominent contribution to the country'; he also won the title of the State Exemplary Workers in Culture, Education and Health Care Sectors, and one of the 100 Best Doctors in China.

Over the past five decades, with rich practical experience and eruditions, he has overcome difficult cases in thoracic and cardiovascular surgery. He was the first in China to perform a surgery for aortic dissecting aneurysm (in April 1982), the Bentall procedure for a Marfan aortic root aneurysm (in March 1985), and a surgery for Budd-Chiari syndrome, all of which have been made available all over the country. He invented limited side-to-side portacaval shunt to treat portal hypertension, which formed an important method of surgical treatment. He has conducted in-depth research on valvular disease accompanied by chronic atrial fibrillation, the protection of isolated donor heart, congenital heart disease, valvular disease and bioprosthetic valve, breaking new grounds in surgery. He has published 205 academic papers and 7 books. He has been the editor-in-chief of monographs such as *Modern Cardiothoracic Surgery, Modern Postoperative Complications Studies, The Treatment and Study of Portal Hypertension*, and *Surgery*, a senior medical textbook. He has received 3 second-level National Prizes for Progress in Science and Technology and 19 provincial and ministerial prizes for his prominent contributions to the development of aortic surgery in China.

Professor Sun is a professional, virtuous and conscientious doctor. Though over eighty years old, he endeavors to serve outpatients, direct difficult surgeries, exam drafts, write books and attend academic meetings. He is still interested in the latest developments in medical science and carries on his research on thoracic and cardiac surgery.

# 序言　　　学为人师 行为世范

　　2009年是中华人民共和国成立60周年，也是孙衍庆教授从医、行医、传医60年。

　　孙衍庆教授是北京安贞医院名誉院长，中华胸心血管外科学会名誉主任委员，北京生物工程学会名誉理事长，首都医科大学胸心血管外科教授，主任医师，硕士、博士及博士后教育流动站导师，北京大学医学部临床医学院客座教授，是我国著名的胸心血管外科专家。

　　孙衍庆教授1949年毕业于北京大学医学院，历任北京友谊医院外科主任，外科教研室主任、副院长，北京市卫生局局长兼党组书记，北京安贞医院院长兼北京市心肺血管中心主任；是北京市有突出贡献的专家，享受国务院政府特殊津贴的专家，中国人民政治协商会议第七、第八届全国委员会委员。先后获得"全国百名优秀医生"、"首都优秀医务工作者"、"北京市卫生系统先进个人"、"北京市优秀共产党员"、中华医学会胸心血管外科分会"杰出贡献奖"、中国医师协会"心血管外科医师终身成就奖"等多项殊荣。

　　60载春华秋实，60载医路漫漫，孙衍庆教授表现出了一个中国优秀知识分子的优良品质和高尚人格。他历经艰难困苦，立志从医报国，积极投身于民族解放、国家振兴和祖国医疗卫生事业；他致力于我国胸心血管外科事业，坚持刻苦钻研，勇攀医学科学高峰，创造了许多治疗疑难杂症的国内首例；他全心对待病人，秉承大医本色，赢得了无数患者的信任与爱戴；他坚持言传身教，悉心提携后人，为国家造就了一批卓有成就的医学科技人才；他为官勤政，廉洁自律，为北京市医疗工作和安贞医院的发展倾注了大量心血。

　　"学为人师，行为世范"，孙衍庆教授无愧为一位医德高尚、医术高超的医学大家，一位认真钻研、技艺精湛的医学科学家，一位著述等身、桃李满天的医学教育家，一位在医疗事业和医院管理上成效卓著的管理专家。

　　孙衍庆教授对理想的追求、对事业的执着和无私奉献、对工作的高度责任感和使命感，使我们深为感动。这是一笔无形的财富，是安贞医院事业蓬勃发展的旗帜。

　　通过这本画册，我们回顾孙衍庆教授的丰富经历和人生历程，展示他的崇高品质和人生价值；同时也促使我们学会思考，思考如何做人、如何做事，提醒我们时刻不忘自己所肩负的职责和重任。

　　大医精诚，止于至善。孙老的高尚品德、严谨态度和坚定信念，将永远激励我们为祖国的医疗卫生事业、为提高人民的健康水平做出新的贡献！

张兆光

二零零九年十月十八日

# Preface
# An Eminent Scholar and Exemplary Teacher

2009 marks the 60th anniversary of the People's Republic of China and also the 60th year of the beginning of Professor Sun Yanqing's career as a doctor and teacher of medicine.

Professor Sun Yanqing is the honorary president of Beijing Anzhen Hospital, the honorary chairman of China Society of Thoracic and Cardiovascular Surgery, the honorary president of the council of Beijing Bioengineering Society, professor and chief physician at the Thoracic and Cardiovascular Surgery Department of Capital University of Medical Science, supervisor of doctoral candidates and centers for post-doctoral studies, and guest professor at the Clinical College of the Faculty of Medical Sciences of Beijing University. He is one of China's preeminent experts of thoracic and cardiovascular surgery.

Professor Sun graduated from the Medical College of Beijing University in 1949. He has successively been head of the surgical department of Beijing Friendship Hospital, director of its Teaching and Research Section of Surgery, its vice president, chief and party secretary of Beijing Public Health Bureau, president of Beijing Anzhen Hospital and director of Beijing Center of Cardio-pulmonary Vessel Diseases. He is one of Beijing's 'experts with prominent contributions', a recipient of special government allowance from the State Council, and a member of the 7th and 8th National Committee of the CPPCC. He was listed among a Hundred Outstanding Doctors all over China, Outstanding Medical Workers in the Capital, Exemplary Individuals in the Healthcare System of Beijing, and Outstanding Communist Party Members of Beijing; he also received the Outstanding Contribution Award from the Thoracic and Cardiovascular Surgery Branch of China Society of Medical Sciences and the Lifetime Achievement Award for a Thoracic and Cardiovascular Surgeon from China Medical Doctor Association.

Over the past six decades, Professor Sun has embodied the exemplary quality and noble character of an eminent Chinese intellectual. Despite hardships, he made up his mind to serve the country by practicing medicine and devoted himself to the national rejuvenation, and the health care undertaking. Dedicated to developing thoracic and cardiovascular surgery in China, he studied hard and worked diligently, making many No.1s in the treatment of the complicated diseases across the country. He has won the trust and respect of numerous patients on account of the wholehearted care he shows as a great doctor. As a teacher he has taught by precept and example and brings up a number of successful medical experts, for the country. As an official, he was self-disciplined, and dedicated to Beijing's health care and the development of Anzhen Hospital.

As an eminent scholar and exemplary teacher, He deserves the designation of a virtuous and great doctor, an assiduous scientific researcher, a medical educator who has written prolifically and has pupils everywhere, and an expert who has achieved prominently in health care and hospital management.

Professor Sun's pursuit of his ideals, his selfless dedication to his carrier, and his high sense of responsibility and mission are deeply moving. This is an intangible asset for the thriving of Anzhen Hospital.

This album reviews Professor Sun's colorful life and displays his noble character and self-fulfillment. In addition, it prompts us to learn how to conduct ourselves and reminds us never to forget our duty and responsibility.

A great doctor acts in good faith and strives for perfection. Professor Sun's noble personality, rigorous attitude, and steadfast faith will always encourage us to contribute more to the country's health care and the improvement the people's health.

October 18th, 2009

# 目 录 Contents

艰难困苦

从医报国

Practicing
medicine to serve
the country despite
the hardships

散作乾坤万里春

忽然一夜清香发

不同桃李混芳尘

冰雪林中著此身

# 一、艰难困苦 从医报国

1923年，孙衍庆出生在山东省烟台市。从童年、少年到青年时期，他和那个年代的中国一样，历经了飘摇、困苦。强国兴邦、改变贫困、制服病魔的理想激励着孙衍庆奋发图强，他毅然地走上了一条学医的道路，义无反顾、执着坚定，最终成就了一代医界大家。

1943年，20岁的孙衍庆考取了北京大学医学院。医学院的功课非常繁重，压力很大。为了挣钱补贴生活，孙衍庆业余时间去做家教、打零工，甚至去拉煤车。生活是艰苦的，但正是青年时期生活的磨练，为他后来适应各种环境、承担繁重的工作打下了基础。

日本投降后，中国正义与非正义的斗争仍在继续。治病必先救国，孙衍庆在刻苦攻读的同时，义无反顾地投身到反对独裁、争取民主的爱国斗争中。1945年，国民党政府将收复区的学生认定为"伪学生"，要甄审他们的学籍和学历。同广大爱国青年一起，孙衍庆愤然而起，参加了争取权利的反甄审运动。1946年12月30日，北平爱国学生发动抗议驻华美军暴行的示威游行，孙衍庆积极投身其中。1947年5月，爱国学生掀起声势浩大的反饥饿、反内战运动，孙衍庆走上街头，参加了在北平举行的"华北学生北平区反饥饿反内战大游行"。

在如火如荼的爱国运动中，孙衍庆坚定了只有共产党、只有社会主义才能救中国的信念。1947年7月，孙衍庆加入中国共产党领导的民主青年同盟，之后于1948年7月光荣地加入了中国共产党。1948年10月，孙衍庆奔赴解放区，投身到民族解放和国家振兴的事业中。

1949年4月，孙衍庆返校复学，并于同年7月毕业。毕业后孙衍庆先后被分配到北大医院、北京市第三医院工作，任住院医师和住院总医师。他和千千万万的中国人民一样，沉浸在新中国成立的喜悦中，迎来了人生中新的起点。

1950年，朝鲜战争爆发。中国人民志愿军雄赳赳、气昂昂跨过鸭绿江，揭开了抗美援朝、保家卫国的序幕。刚刚参加工作的孙衍庆积极参加了抗美援朝医疗队，成为北京市第一批医疗队队员，满腔热血地奔赴前线，抢救伤病员、经受考验、立功受奖。

1951年冬，孙衍庆从医疗队回到北京，随即参加了前苏联援建项目——苏联红十字医院的筹建工作。

青年时期的孙衍庆把自己的命运与国家民族的命运紧紧联系起来，这种以国家兴亡、民族兴衰为己任，无畏艰苦、执着追求真理的世界观和价值观也深深地影响了他的一生。

# I. Practicing medicine to serve the country despite the hardships

In 1923, Sun Yanqing was born in Yantai, Shandong. His childhood, adolescence and youth were marked by unstableness and hardships. The ideals of making the country powerful and prosperous, lifting it out of poverty and overcome diseases encouraged him to take up medicine. Eventually, his resolution and perseverance made him a master of medical science.

In 1943, at the age of twenty, Sun was admitted by the Medical College of Beijing University. Despite the heavy pressure from the strenuous courses, he spent his spare time tutoring, doing odd jobs and even pulling coal carts to make ends meet. It was a hard life, but it prepared him for all kinds of environment and onerous tasks.

After Japan surrendered, the war between justice and injustice continued in China. Saving lives must be preceded by saving the country. While studying assiduously, he devoted himself to patriotic movements against dictatorship and for democracy. In 1945, the Nationalist government labeled the students in the former Japanese-occupied areas 'students under the puppet government' and attempted to screen them for their status as students and record of formal schooling. Together with patriotic young people stirred by indignation, Sun joined in the anti-screening movement claiming their rights. On December 30, 1946, patriotic students in Peking staged a demonstration against the atrocities of U.S. troops in China, and Sun played an active part in it. In May 1947, patriotic students launched a massive movement against hunger and the civil war. Sun went to the street to join in the Demonstration against Hunger and the Civil War by North China Students in Peking.

The patriotic movements that swept the country like a raging fire convinced him that only the communist party and socialism could save China. In July 1947, he joined the Alliance of Young Democrats led by the Chinese Communist Party. In 1948, he joined the Party. In October 1948, he went to the liberated area to contribute to national liberation and reinvigoration.

In April 1949, he returned to college to resume his studies. After his graduation in July, he was assigned to work in Beijing University Hospital first and then to the Third Hospital of Beijing as resident doctor and later as chief resident doctor. Like millions of Chinese people, he was overjoyed by the founding of the People's Republic of China, which marked a new starting point in his life.

In 1950, the Korean War broke out. The Chinese People's Volunteer Army crossed the Yalu River to fight against the American army in support of North Korea and defense of China. Having just begun to work, Sun voluntarily joined the PLA medical teams heading for the battlefield and became a member of the first medical teams sent by the city of Beijing. He arrived at the frontier and rescued wounded and sick soldiers from the battlefield. He withstood the test and was rewarded for his meritorious service.

In the winter of 1951, Sun left the medical team and returned to Beijing. Soon afterwards, he joined the preparation for establishing the Soviet Red Cross Hospital, a Russia-assisted project.

In his youth, Sun forged a close link between his destiny and that of the country and the nation. Such world view and values, with concern for the destiny of the country and the nation, no fear for hardships, and persistent pursuit of the truth, had a deep impact on his whole life.

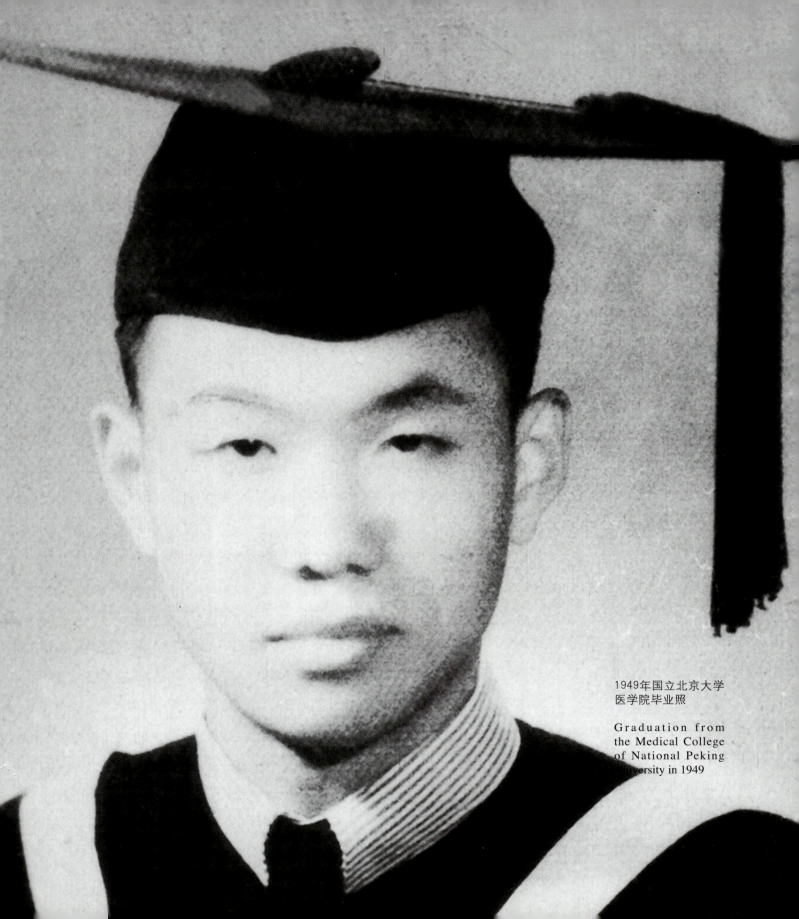

艰难困苦 从医报国 Practicing medicine to serve the country despite the hardships

1949年国立北京大学
医学院毕业照

Graduation from
the Medical College
of National Peking
University in 1949

4

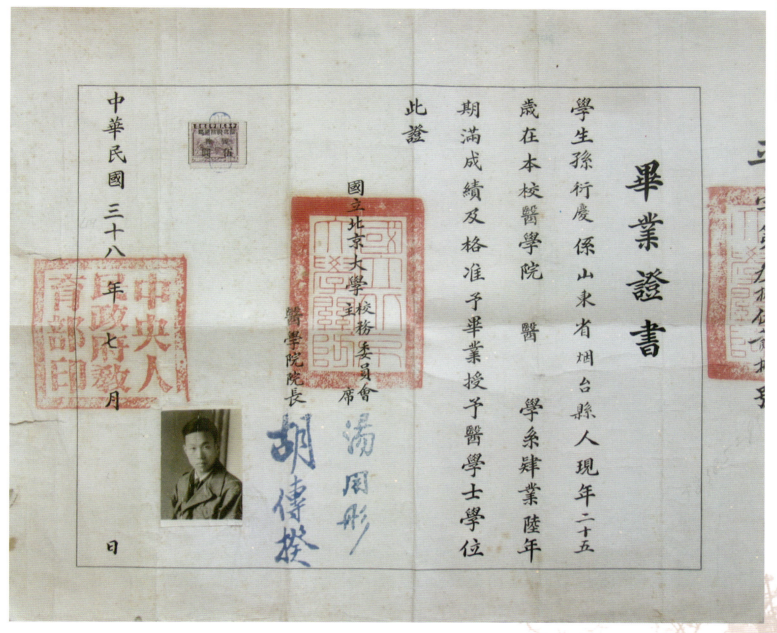

畢業證書

學生孫衍慶係山東省烟台縣人現年二十五
歲在本校醫學院　醫　學系肆業陸年
期滿成績及格准予畢業授予醫學士學位
此證

國立北京大學校務委員會主席　湯用彤
醫學院院長　胡傳揆

中華民國三十八年政府敎月　日

国立北京大学毕业证书
Certificate of graduation from the National Peking University

艰难困苦　从医报国

Practicing medicine to serve the country despite the hardships

府右街北京大学医学院宿舍与进步同学合影
（左三为孙衍庆教授）

With progressive students at the dormitory of the Medical College of Peking University on Fuyou Street (Prof. Sun Yanqing is the third from the left)

北京市西单背阴胡同北京大学医学院附属医院1949年毕业班合影（中间为孙衍庆教授）

The class that graduated in 1949 from the hospital attached to the Medical College of Peking University at Beiyin Alley in Xidan, Beijing; in the middle is Prof. Sun Yanqing

艰难困苦 从医报国

Practicing medicine to serve the country despite the hardships

参加反甄审学生运动

Participation in the anti-screening student movement

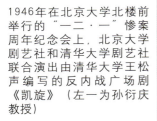

1946年在北京大学北楼前举行的"一二·一"惨案周年纪念会上,北京大学剧艺社和清华大学剧艺社联合演出由清华大学王松声编写的反内战广场剧《凯旋》(左一为孙衍庆教授)

In 1946, at the anniversary meeting of the December 1st Massacre held in front of the North Building of Peking University, the Theatrical Society of Peking University and of Tsinghua University performed *Triumphant Return*, a square drama against the civil war, written by Wang Songsheng from Tsinghua University(Prof. Sun Yanqing is the first of the left)

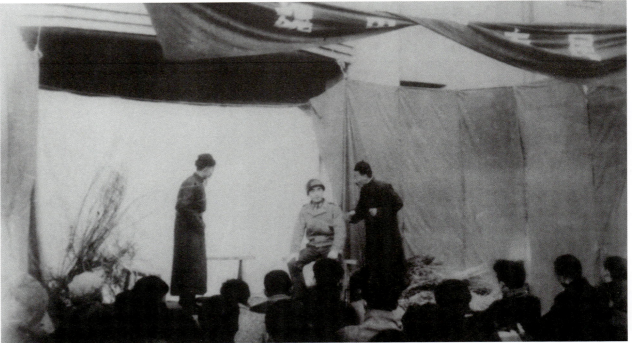

与进步同学合影（左一为孙衍庆教授）
With progressive students (the first on the left is Prof.Sun Yanqing)

1953年北京前苏联红十字医院建院全体医护人员合影

The medical staff of former Soviet Union Red Cross Hospital of Beijing at its establishment ceremony in 1953

在前苏联红十字医院与前苏联专家合影（后排左四为孙衍庆教授）

With former Soviet experts at Soviet Red Cross Hospital(the fourth from the left in the back row is Prof. Sun Yanqing)

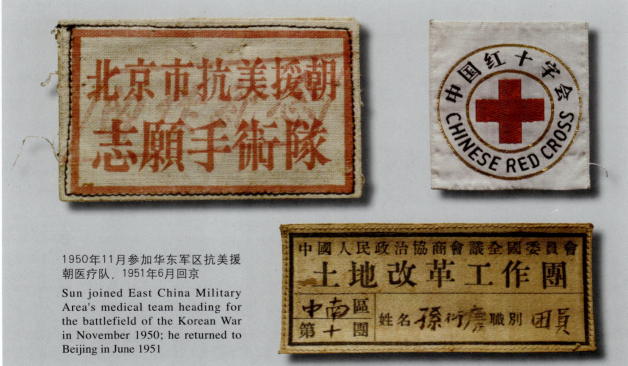

参加中国红十字会议的证章

ID badge for attending the China Red Cross Conference

1950年11月参加华东军区抗美援朝医疗队，1951年6月回京

Sun joined East China Military Area's medical team heading for the battlefield of the Korean War in November 1950; he returned to Beijing in June 1951

1950年批准参加土地改革工作团

Approved for joining the Land Reform Group in 1950

11

艰难困苦 从医报国

Practicing medicine to serve the country despite the hardships

庆祝北医成立70周年医学系49届校友返校留影（后排左五为孙衍庆教授）

The 1949-batch schoolmates of the Medical College at the celebration of the 70th anniversary of Beijing Medical University (the fifth from the left in the back row is Prof.Sun Yanqing)

1989年1月28日纪念北平和平解放40周年座谈会合影（四排左五为孙衍庆教授）

Forum for celebrating the 40th anniversary of the peaceful liberation of Beijing on January 28th, 1989 (the fifth from the left in the fourth row is Prof.Sun Yanqing)

1964年10月5日党和国家领导人接见国庆15周年全国劳模代表合影
Representatives of national model workers photographed on the 15th National Day

咬定青山不放松，立根原在破岩中。千磨万击还坚劲，任尔东西南北风。

业精于勤

Practice makes
perfect

玉汝于成

咬定青山不放松

# 二、业精于勤　玉汝于成

医生面对的对象是人，是人的生命，真正的医学大家背后是艰苦的劳动和超人的付出。孙衍庆以勤奋为基石，以高度的责任心在医学的世界里执着前行。

在六年的大学时间里，孙衍庆刻苦攻读、成绩优良，打下了扎实的专业基础。他重视积累实践经验，早年从事过普外科、骨科、创伤、肝胆外科和胸心血管外科的病房和门诊工作，也做过麻醉、泌尿等多方面工作。他后来在胸心血管外科的成就，与这样一个广泛的外科基础密不可分。1964年，孙衍庆作为劳动模范国庆观礼代表，受到了毛泽东、刘少奇、朱德、周恩来等党和国家领导人的亲切接见。

医学无捷径，钻研和学习是获得成功的唯一道路。临床医生日常工作繁忙、疲于应付，时间总是不够用，容易忽略读书和研究新问题。长此以往得不到系统的提高，很容易人云亦云、没有建树，难以形成一家之长。孙衍庆教授以"勤奋"二字解决了这一矛盾。无数个休息日他都在图书馆内查阅文献，绘制手术图，书写了5000余张资料卡片；许多个深夜他都在苦苦求索中度过，积累了深厚的医学基础功底和广博的知识。

为了开展心脏血管外科手术，孙衍庆经常几个月内天天晚上都在实验室内研究心肺机的结构，进行动物实验，研究心脏停跳和复跳的规律，有时还要精心制作特用的手术器械。限制性门腔静脉侧侧分流术专用器械，人工瓣膜替换的基本技术也是在这样的日日夜夜内反复制作与研究中取得成功的。

在医疗工作中不断积累、开拓前进，孙衍庆用精湛的技术、智慧和魄力创造了许多疑难杂症的国内首例：

首例报告主动脉夹层动脉瘤根治手术（1982.4）；

首例报告马凡综合征主动脉根部瘤根治手术（Bentall 1985.3）；

首例布加氏综合征经后腹腔右心房下腔静脉转流术；

首例锁骨下动脉窃血综合征手术治疗；

创建了限制性门腔静脉侧侧分流术的理论和方法。

此外，他对瓣膜病伴发慢性房颤、巨左房症外科治疗、离体供心保护、先心病、瓣膜病和人工生物瓣膜等多方面也进行了深入研究，开拓了新手术领域。

孙衍庆经常提到前苏联专家纳格尼别达的名字，把他奉为自己从医路上的导师。这位当年在原苏联红十字医院与孙衍庆共事的专家曾对他说："临床医生不仅要治好病，还要教会人们预防疾病；最重要的是不能只做外科技匠，一定要做医学研究，做推动医学科学进步与发展的医学科学家。"这句话对孙衍庆今后的医疗工作产生了极大的影响。

他不满足于只成为一名成功的"外科技匠"，而重视积累临床经验、专业理论，刻苦钻研中外医学经典著作，向名专家请教，并提出一些思考性的问题。这些都为孙衍庆教授成为一名医学大家奠定了坚实的基础。

## II. Practice makes perfect

A doctor's job is to save human lives. To be a great doctor calls for arduous toil and extraordinary efforts. Sun forged ahead in the world of medical science with industry and an acute sense of responsibility.

His assiduous study during the six years in college gave him outstanding grades and a solid foundation in his major. Setting store by practical experience, he worked in wards and outpatient departments of general surgery, orthopedics, traumatology, hepatobiliary surgery, and thoracic and cardiovascular surgery; he also worked in other fields, such as anesthesia and urology. His later achievements in thoracic and cardiovascular surgery would have been impossible without such an extensive training in surgery. At the ceremony of the National Day in 1964, he was received as a model worker by leaders of the Party and the state, including Mao Zedong, Liu Shaoqi, Zhu De and Zhou Enlai.

There's no short cuts for practicing medicine. Study and learning are the only way to success. Because of their heavy workload and tight schedule, clinical doctors are likely to ignore the importance of reading and exploring new issues. If this continues for long, the lack of systematic improvement will deprive them of the ability of independent thinking and prevent them from achieving anything special. Sun solved the problem with diligence. He spent numerous holidays consulting data in libraries, drawing surgery charts, and writing over 5,000 data cards. He passed many small hours in contemplation, cultivating a profound basis and an erudite learning.

In order to perform cardiovascular surgery, Sun spent almost every night of several months in the lab examining the structure of the heart-lung machine, making experiments on animals, studying the law of cardiac arrest and resuscitation, and sometimes making specialized surgical instruments. The instruments for restrictive portacaval shunt and the basic technique for prosthetic valve replacement were successfully developed in this way.

As he continuously accumulated experience and forged ahead, his superb skills, intelligence and daring made him the first in China to overcome many difficult cases:

He was reported to be the first to perform radical surgery for aortic dissecting aneurysm (April 1982), the first to perform Bentall procedure for a Marfan aortic root aneurysm February 1985, the first to perform right atrium inferior vena cava bypass through retroperitoneal for Budd-Chiari Syndrome, and the first to perform surgery for subclavian steal phenomenon.

He established the theory and method of restrictive portacaval shunt.

He has also made in-depth research into valvular disease accompanied by chronic atrial fibrillation, surgery for giant left atrium, the protection of isolated donor heart, congenital heart disease, and valvular disease and bioprosthetic valve, breaking new grounds in surgery.

Sun frequently mentions former Soviet expert Nagnibeda, whom he regards as his mentor. The expert, who used to be his colleage at the former Soviet Red Cross Hospital, said to him, 'A clinical doctor must not only cure diseases but also teach people to prevent them. Most importantly, he must not be nothing more than a surgical craftsman; instead, he must do medical research and be a medical scientist contributing to the progress of medical science.' That remark had tremendous impact on Sun's career.

Not content with being a successful 'surgical craftsman', he set store by accumulating clinical experience and professional theories, perused Chinese and foreign medical classics, consulted eminent experts, and raised thought-provoking questions. All these paved the way for his becoming a master of medical science.

业精于勤 玉汝于成 Practice makes perfect

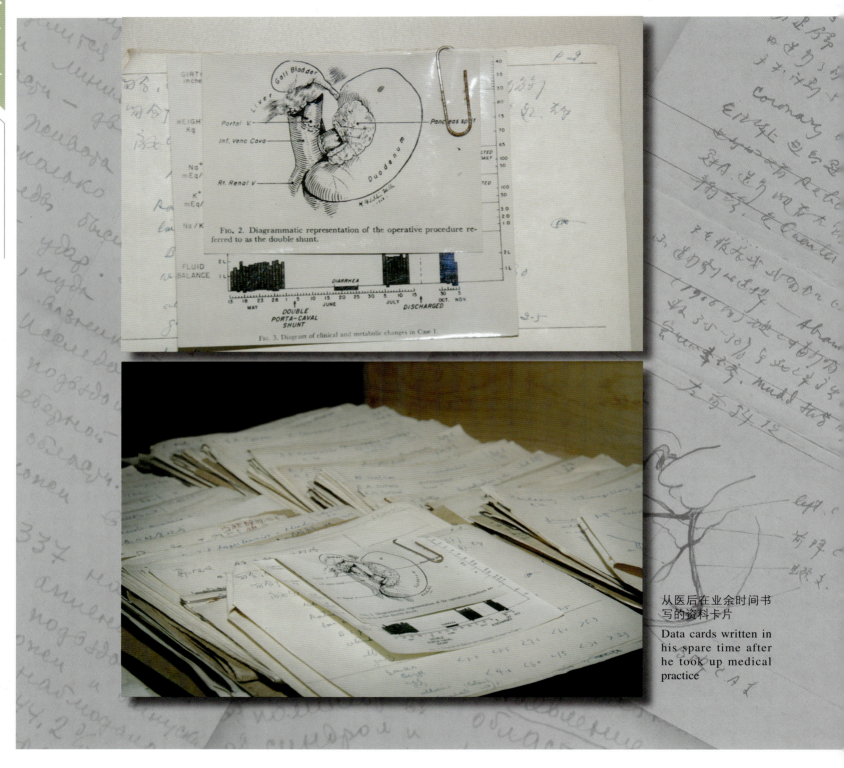

从医后在业余时间书写的资料卡片

Data cards written in his spare time after he took up medical practice

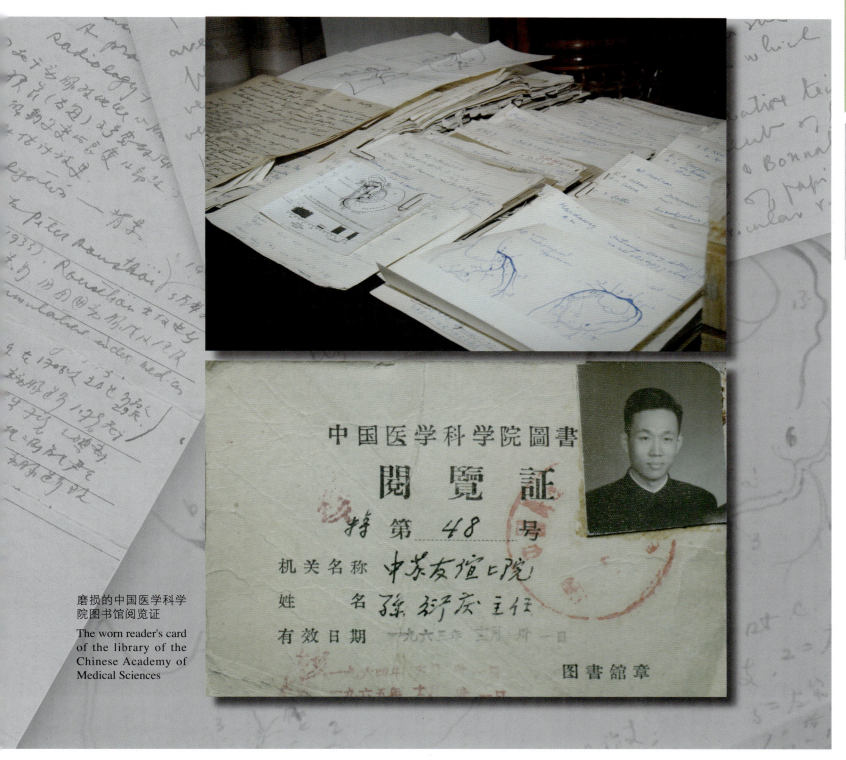

磨损的中国医学科学
院图书馆阅览证

The worn reader's card
of the library of the
Chinese Academy of
Medical Sciences

业精于勤 玉汝于成 Practice makes perfect

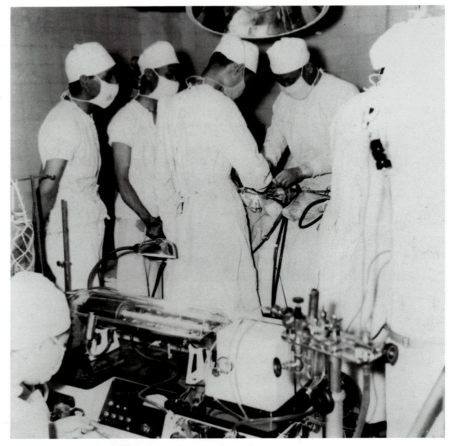

20世纪50年代末使用的体外循环设备

CPB device used in the late 1950s

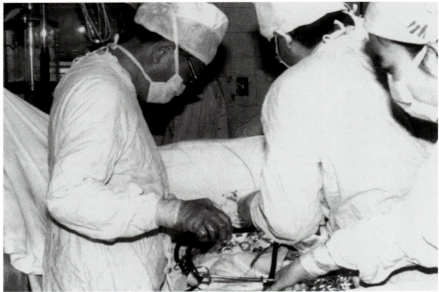

1982年首例主动脉夹层动脉瘤手术

The first surgery for aortic dissecting aneurysm in 1982

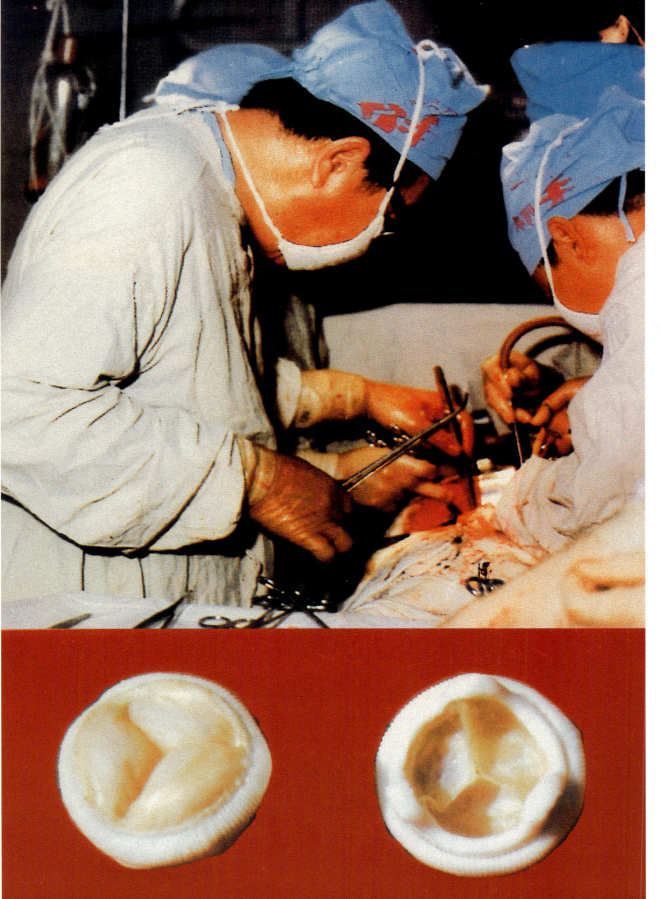

业精于勤 玉汝于成 Practice makes perfect

孙衍庆教授在用自制生物人工瓣膜进行二尖瓣替换术（下图为自制适度低架生物瓣）

Prof. Sun was performing the mitral valve replacement with homemade bioprosthetic valve. The picture below is the homemade moderate low-bed bioprosthetic valve

业精于勤 玉汝于成 Practice makes perfect

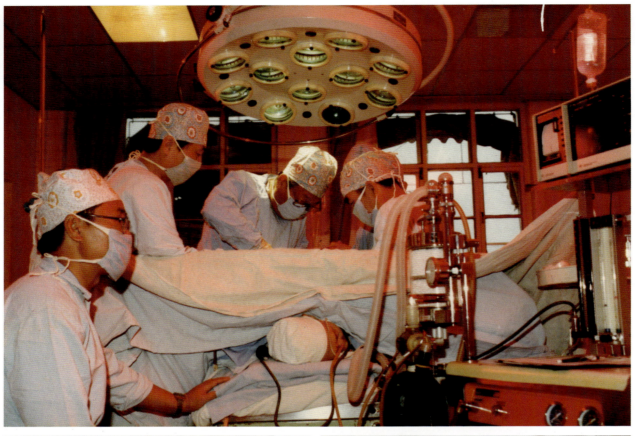

孙衍庆教授在进行人工心脏瓣膜双瓣替换手术

Prof.Sun Yanqing was performing double valve replacement for artificial heart valve

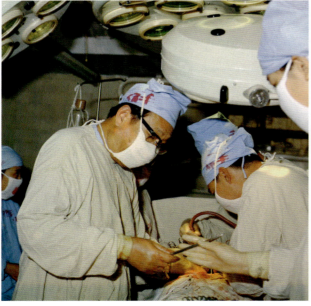

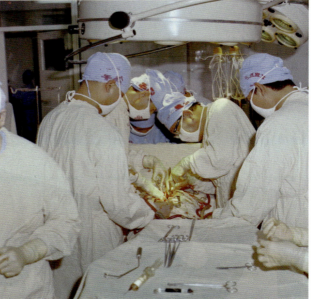

友谊医院手术照片

Performing operations at Friendship Hospital

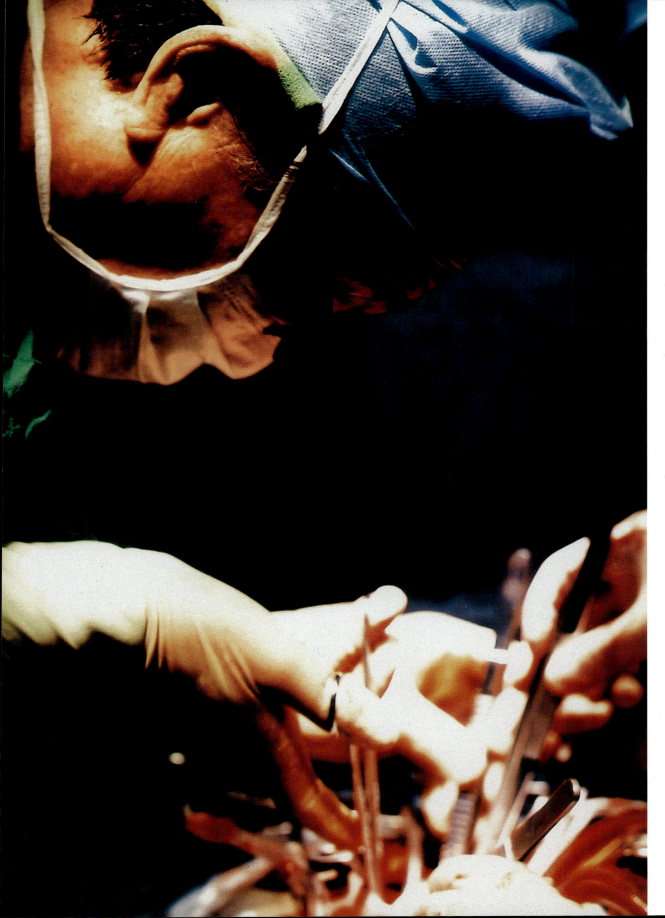

1985年孙衍庆教授在做马凡综合征主动脉根部瘤根治手术

Prof. Sun Yanqing was performing Bentall procedure for Marfan aortic root aneurysm.

孙衍庆

业精于勤　玉汝于成

Practice makes perfect

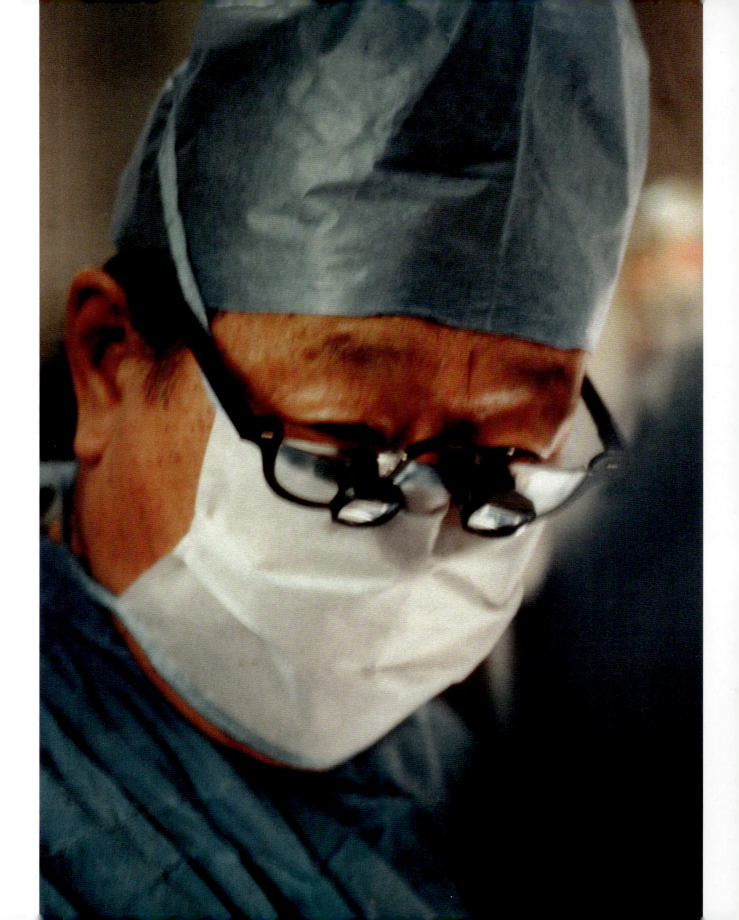

凝视
Gazing

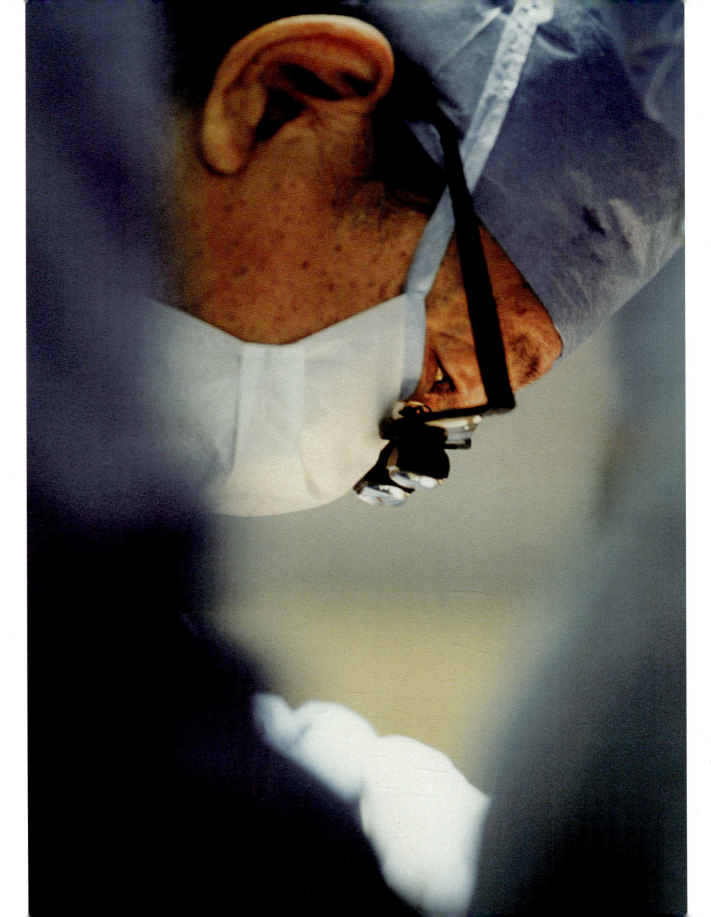

业精于勤 玉汝于成 Practice makes perfect

专注
Absorption

27

孙衍庆

业精于勤 玉汝于成 Practice makes perfect

志存高远　严谨治学

Lofty ideals and rigorous
attitude

认真整理论文资料
Carefully sorting out data for academic papers

三次获得国家科技进步奖

Prof. Sun has received the National Award for Progress in Science and Technology for three times

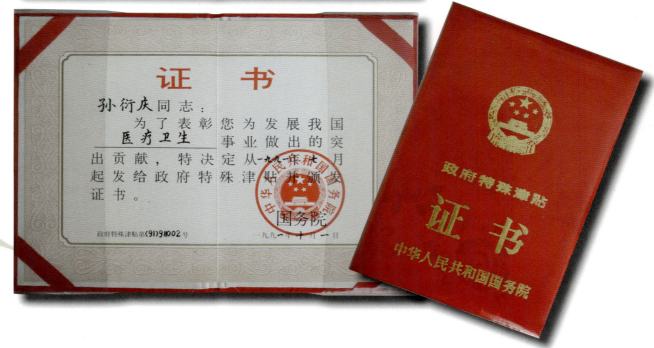

北京市科学技术奖

荣誉证书

北京市人民政府

荣誉證書

北京市人民政府

荣誉证书

北京市科学技术进步奖

北京市人民政府

荣誉证书

北京市科学技术进步奖

北京市人民政府

孙衍庆 同志:

升主动脉瘤伴主动脉瓣关闭不全的临床研究 获得北京市科学技术进步奖 壹 等奖 你在该项工作中做出了成绩特授予此证书

北京市科学技术进步奖评审委员会

一九九〇年三月

硕果累累

Fruitful research

1995年4月国家科技进步奖、发明奖评审会专家合影（前排左四为孙衍庆教授）

Experts of the evaluation panel for National Science and Technology Award and National Invention Award in April 1995

业精于勤 玉汝于成 Practice makes perfect

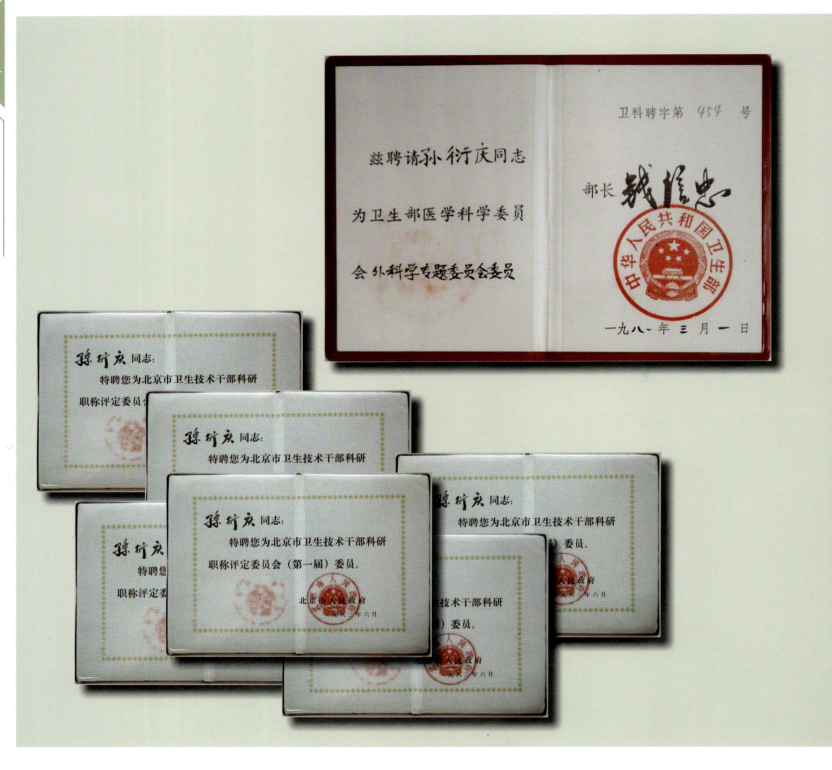

成绩斐然
Brilliant achievements

折荇聊可佩
入室自成芳
開花不竟笄
含秀委微霜

仁之孝德

Great virtue and
benevolence

境界至臻

## 三、仁心厚德　境界至臻

有一句古语：德不近佛者不可以为医，才不近仙者不可以为医，孙衍庆对病人有着极度的热忱。他爱病人，尊重病人，处处为病人着想，深谙和谐医患关系之道。

他尊重病人，首先是极为耐心、认真地倾听病人陈述病情，对病情有了诊断意见后，他以温和体贴的语言向病人介绍清楚，包括治疗意见和手术方案也是仔细听取病人和家属的意见。尊重病人，更是尊重病人的生命。他对急、难、重的病人在术前、术中和术后可能发生的问题；以及如何应对这些问题加强对病人的保护，不使之受损或产生并发症，以及术后如何保持病人有较高的生存质量等，都在制定手术方案中考虑周到，再极为精心地施行手术。

他很注意细节，对每一位病人和每个治疗方案都认真观察思考，力求诊断、治疗、手术都做得十分规范与全面。在他领导的手术室内，手术过程总是静悄悄地、井然有序地进行，没有任何干扰。在门诊和查房时，他面对病人说话和气、诚恳、柔和，着装整洁得体，环境文明干净。讲究礼仪，温文尔雅，不急不躁，表现出他作为一名医生应有的文化修养。

孙衍庆查房非常有特点，用两个字概括的话就是"严谨"。每次查房，他都悉心询问病情，认真检查病人，不放过一丝一毫可疑的体征，每个数据都力求准确。在他看来，只要和病人有关，任何事情都来不得半点马虎。

在孙衍庆的眼中，医生的职业就是救死扶伤，医生与患者之间的关系不是用金钱来衡量的，真诚互信才是医患关系和谐的根本所在。在他的办公室里有不同的病人送给他的牌匾，写满了感谢的话语，也写满了病人对他发自内心的感激。

学习、行医60年，孙衍庆遇到了很多让他感动的患者，医患之间的真情成为推动他不断努力的力量源泉。

20世纪50年代，毕业时间不长的孙衍庆为一名食道烧伤的7岁外地男孩进行了人工食管手术。25年后，这位已成长为壮年男子的患者带着妻女历尽周折，出现在孙衍庆面前，执意让他收下一个生日蛋糕："今天我来，就是想让您看看您带给我的幸福。我长大了，娶妻生女了，我们全家永远忘不了您。"

25年间孙衍庆已经转战北大医院、北京市第三医院、北京友谊医院、北京安贞医院等多家医疗机构，治疗过的患者不计其数。面对千方百计寻找到他的这名"患儿"，孙衍庆称"此情此景牢牢地映入脑海，再也不能忘却。"

# III. Great virtue and benevolence

An old saying goes that one cannot be a doctor without Buddha-like virtue and god-like talent. Sun is extremely devoted to his patients and considerate of their needs, loving them and respecting them. Over the years, he has learned the art of forging a harmonious relationship with patients.

His respect for patients is expressed in many ways. First of all, he listens to the patient very patiently and carefully as the latter recounts his condition. Having made a diagnosis, he presents it to the patient in a gentle and considerate tone. He listens attentively to the opinions of the patient and his family to decide on the treatment or the plan of surgery. Moreover, he respects the patient's life. When he draws up a plan of surgery, he takes into consideration the problems that may occur before, during and after the operations on a patient with an acute, difficult or grave disease, the method of dealing with the problems and improving the protection of the patient from injury and complications, and the maintenance of a relatively high quality of life after the operation. Then he performs the surgery with utmost care.

He is attentive to details. He carefully observes and thinks about every patient and every plan of treatment, trying to strictly follow the standard and see the whole picture in diagnosis, treatment and surgery. In the operation rooms supervised by him, operations always proceed quietly and in good order, without any disturbance. When receiving outpatients and going the rounds of the wards, he speaks to patients kindly, gently and sincerely. His neat dress, clean office and courteous manners show the refinement a doctor is supposed to have.

His ward round is characterized by rigorousness. Each time, he asks patients about their condition in detail and carefully examines them, not overlooking the vaguest suspicious sign and demanding absolute precision for all data. In his eye, anything concerning patients calls for the utmost attention.

In his opinion, a doctor's job is to cure diseases and save lives; the relationship between a doctor and his patients cannot be measured in terms of money, and the key to a harmonious relationship is sincerity and mutual trust between them. His office features tablets given by his patients, who expressed their heartfelt gratitude with the words on them.

Over the past six decades in which he studied and practiced medicine, Sun has met many patients that moved him. The sincere feelings between him and his patients and the gratitude of the latter have been the source of his unflagging industry.

In the 1950s, when he graduated from college for not a long time, Sun installed an artificial esophagus on a seven-year-old boy from outside Beijing who had had his esophagus burnt. Twenty-five years go, the patient, who had grown into a young man in his prime, found Sun with his wife and daughter despite all the difficulties and insisted that he accept a birthday cake. The man said, "The reason why I came here is that I want you to see the happiness you brought to me. I have grown up, married and had a daughter. My family will never forget you."

During the twenty-five years, Sun had successively transferred to Beijing University Hospital, the Third Hospital of Beijing, Beijing Friendship Hospital and Beijing Anzhen University, and had treated innumerable patients. According to him, he will never forget the day when he met the former little patient who had tried every means to find him.

任友谊医院外科主任时
的孙衍庆教授

At a time when he was
head of the Surgical
Department of Friendship
Hospital

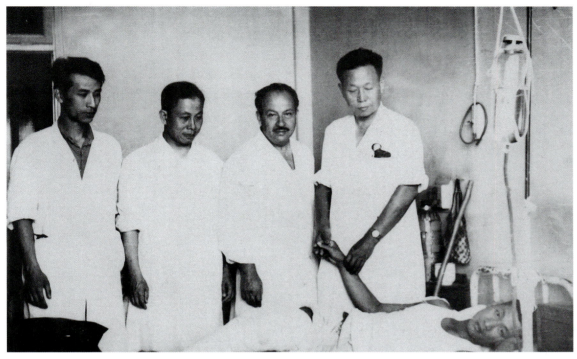

在友谊医院与外国
专家共同查房

Going the rounds of
the wards with foreign
experts at Friendship
Hospital

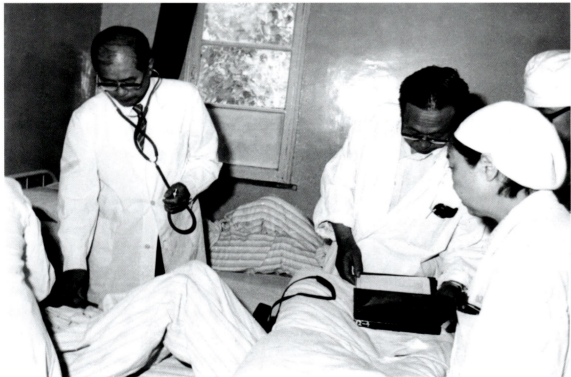

友谊医院查房中仔细
查看病历

Closely examining
a case history when
going the rounds of the
wards at Friendship
Hospital

孙衍庆

仁心厚德 境界至臻

Great virtue and benevolence

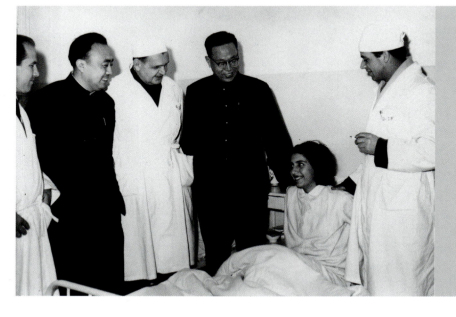

Profesorit të nderuar Sun

Në shenjë kujtimi dhe mirë-
njohjeje të thellë, mjekut të
shquar e të talentuar kinez, i
cili me rastin e ndodhjes në
Shqipëri, me gatishmërinë prej
internacionalisti dhe humanist
të madh pranoi të më bëjë një
operacion shumë të rëndë që
për herë të parë bëhet në
Shqipëri, dhe me mjeshtrinë e
tij prej kirurgu artist, më
shpëtoi jetën!

Adriana Stillo

nxënëse e kl. VIII
shkolla "Kongresi i Përmetit„
Tiranë - SHQIPERI
23·2·1972

1972年赴阿尔巴尼亚
采用限制性门腔静脉
分流术治疗门脉高压
症病人

Treating patients of portal hypertension with restrictive portacaval shunt in Albania in 1972

感谢信译文：送给尊敬的孙教授，以纪念和深切地感激优秀的、有才能的中国医生在阿尔巴尼亚逗留期间以伟大的国际主义和人道主义精神为我做了一个在阿尔巴尼亚首次进行的大手术，并以一名卓越外科医生的技能拯救了我的生命。

与阿尔巴尼亚医生交流

Comparing notes with Albanian doctors

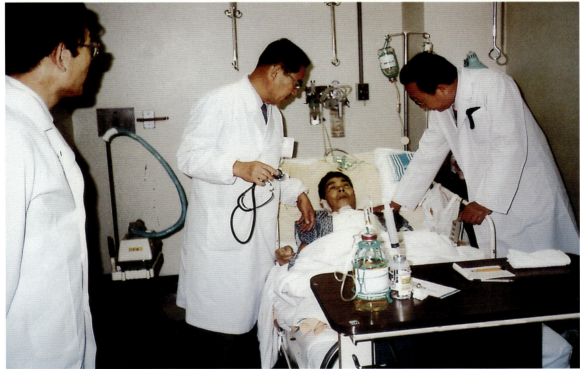

坚持查房

Persisting in going the rounds of the wards

47

仁心厚德 境界至臻

Great virtue and benevolence

12年前白祖诚先生在安贞医院住院，孙教授为他做了心脏手术，康复后白先生潜心写作了200多万字的著作

Twelve years ago Prof. Sun performed a heart surgery on Bai Zucheng at Anzhen Hospital; after recuperation, Mr. Bai devoted himself to writing for a decade and published books with over 2 million characters

1989年在非洲义诊

Offering free medical service in Africa in 1989

2002年79岁高龄仍参加义诊

Still Offering free medical service at the age of 79 in 2002

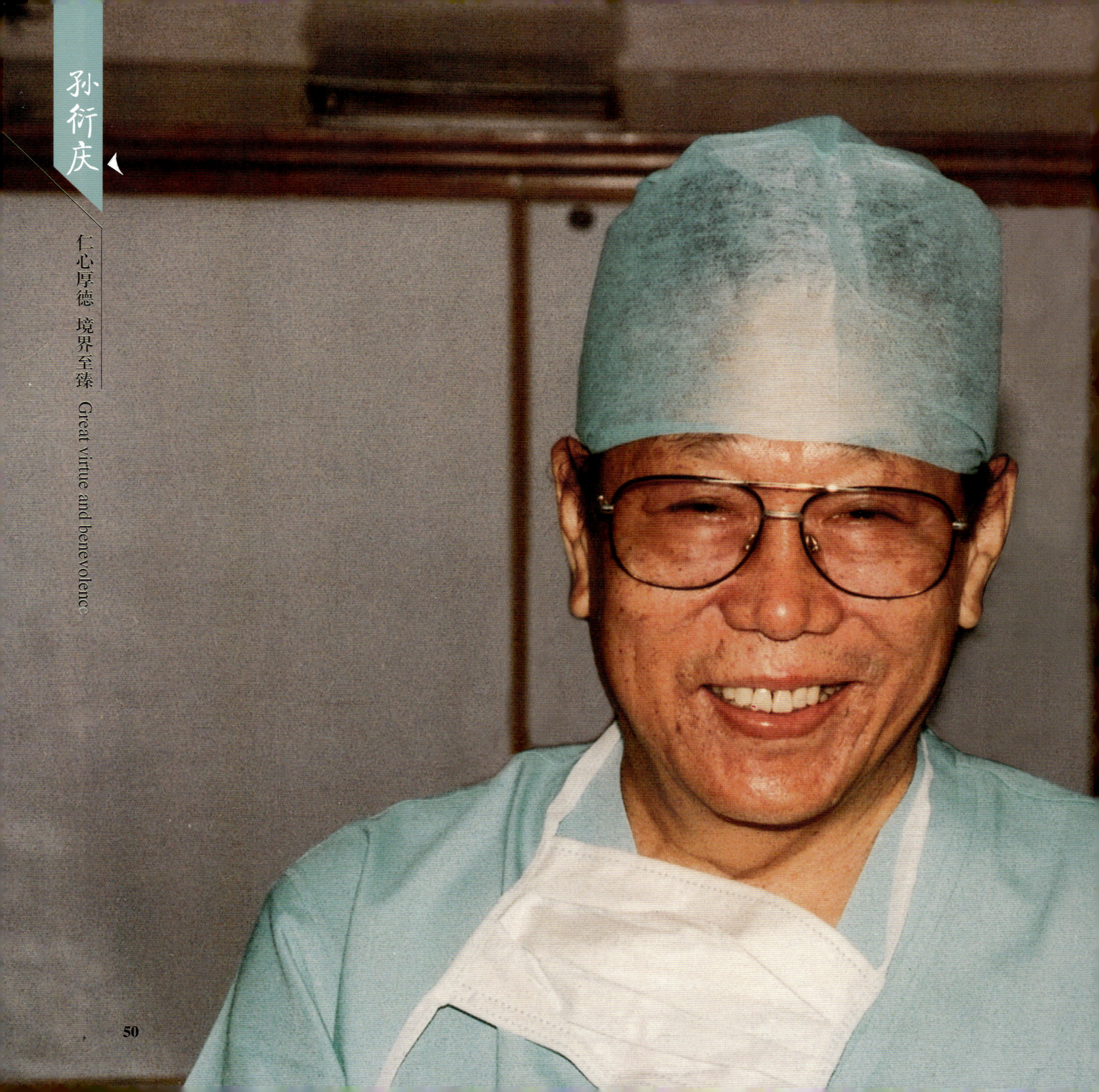

2001年78岁高龄的孙
教授仍然坚持手术

Performing surgery at
the age of 78 in 2001

收获感激
Receiving gratitudes

敬颂孙衍庆院长

老驥優櫪 志在千里
蓋世一刀 堪稱神醫

河北省南宫市教育局户庆海
一九九九年九月九日

孙衍庆同志当选为：

全国百名优秀医生

中华医学会
中华医院管理学会
《健康报》社
1999年2月

孙衍庆院长

恩 人

中法瑪睿尔工业有限公司 吴连科
中国石化北京石化工程公司 周 洁
二000年十月二十日

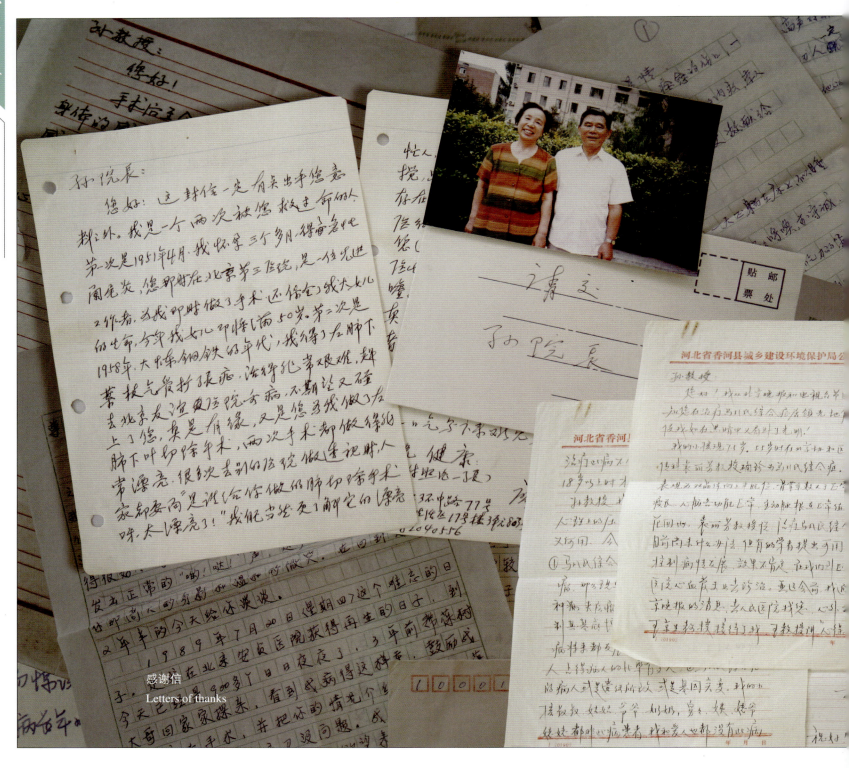

感谢信
Letters of thanks

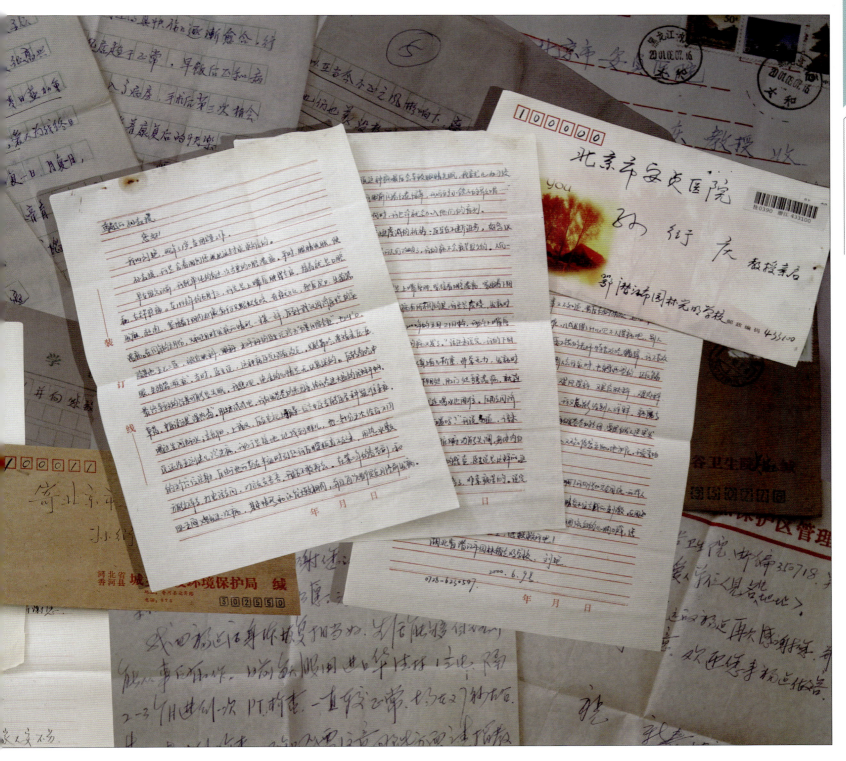

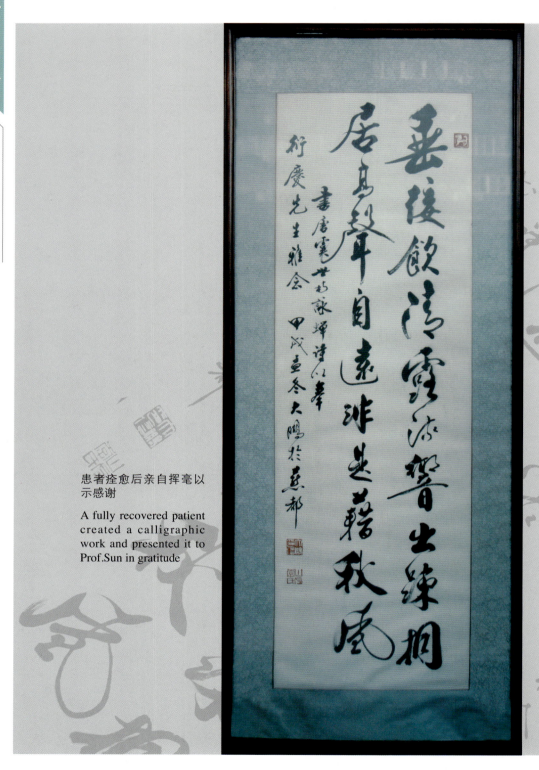

患者痊愈后亲自挥毫以
示感谢

A fully recovered patient
created a calligraphic
work and presented it to
Prof.Sun in gratitude

垂缕饮清露，流响出疏
桐。居高声自远，非是
藉秋风。

He drinks the dew, and
sings among the sparse
Chinese parasol trees. His
voice is heard from afar,
not because of the autumn
wind, but because of his
lofty position.

**56**

衍庆兄从医半个多世纪，悬壶济世，救治病人成千上万，医术精湛，医德高尚，深得病家之爱戴。近十年来，我辈同年，陆续退养山林，兄已逾古稀之高龄，老而弥坚，壮心不已，勇攀高峰，硕果累累，真后辈之楷模也。今喜逢吾兄七五华诞，恭录杜甫诗《望岳》句，奉贺。衍庆吾兄方家雅正。

弟刘呈瑜敬题

The main idea of the colligraphic work: My friend Yanqing, who has practiced medicine for over half a century, has treated and cured tens of thousands of patients. He is held in high esteem by patients for his outstanding expertise and virtue. In the past decade, my peers have retired one by one. However, though over seventy years old, he has retained his resolve, ambition and persistence, which have yielded ample results and made him an example for doctors of the younger generations. Now, at his 75th birthday, I have respectfully copied lines from Viewing Mount Tai by Du Fu in congratulation.

Liu Chengyu

直荷素秋霜色裹

自甘孤处作孤芳

教 学 相 长

弦歌不輟

**A lasting teaching career**

不学渊范仕艳阳 东篱黄菊为谁香

## 四、教学相长　弦歌不辍

　　从20世纪60年代开始，孙衍庆就兼职首都医科大学的临床医学主任，主持教学，经常为学生讲课；还兼任过北京医科大学的临床学院客座教授，并担任3名硕士、10名博士研究生和2名博士后的导师。

　　孙衍庆教授特别重视为国家培养优秀医学人才。他在医生、科主任岗位上，在大学讲台上，为国家培养了一批很有成就的科技人才。"争取多出成果、多出人才"是他最大的心愿。为此，他悉心培养、严格要求青年医师和研究生，无论年龄大小均以诚相待，手把手地教。他对学生的培养不仅停留在提高他们的临床能力，更善于挖掘、尊重和发挥每个人的特长，随时把临床问题提升为科研项目的思路，指导学生把注意力投向更高的层次，解决临床工作中更需要突破的难题。在他的指导下，一批批中青年专业人才脱颖而出。

　　2003年毕业的博士后研究生张宏家已是主任医师，领导临床工作，现在任安贞医院科研处处长，并继续进行夹层动脉瘤的研究。博士蔺嫦燕已是生物医学工程研究室主任，并担任北京市科技新星课题负责人。博士屈正任医院试验室主任，研究的激光治疗冠心病的动物实验与临床应用成果已列入朱晓东主编的《心脏外科学》，是科技新星课题负责人。博士刘愚勇认真负责地进行科研和临床工作，获得病人的赞誉。博士谢进生深入研究马凡的遗传基因和治疗问题。博士侯晓彤是灌注科主任医师，安贞医院体外循环科副主任。博士后江朝光现在任解放军总医院科研处长。博士杨传瑞担任友谊医院心脏研究中心主任，发挥着主力作用……

　　老师的言传身教，传递着医者之魂。在孙衍庆看来，医学教师是个神圣的工作，拥有重大的责任。传授医学知识只是其中的一部分，作为一名医生、一名老师，更应当将崇高的医德、良好的医风传授于学生，让学生明白"健康所系、性命相托"誓言的真谛。

　　他多次严肃地对学生们讲："作为外科医学家，道德观的内涵究竟是什么？应该这样认识的：在治愈的基础上，最大限度地保留患者的健康器官与组织，不需切除的不切除；在有经验的医生指导下进行手术，既保证病人安全，又能达到学习与提高的目的，切不可在没有足够的经验和把握的情况下上台。我们手中的刀维系一个人的生命和一个家庭的幸福。在关键时刻还要敢与病人共同承担手术的风险，在术前要充分估计、分析、判断手术治疗与药物保守治疗的优劣，以决定是否手术；关心指导病人手术前后的生活与健康，最大限度地提高病人术后的生活质量；正确对待病人的感激，应把这些作为努力学习、提高外科技术，更好地维护人类健康的力量源泉。真正的医生还要敢为病人担风险。"

　　孙老的众多研究生对自己的导师充满了崇敬之情。用他们的话说"孙院长不仅教我们做学问，同时教我们怎样做人、做事"。

# IV. A lasting teaching career

In the 1960s, Sun Yanqing began to serve concurrently as the dean of clinical medicine at Capital University of Medical Sciences, supervising teaching and frequently lecturing students. He was also a guest professor at the clinical college of Beijing Medical University, and the supervisor of three postgraduates, ten doctoral candidates, and two postdoctoral students.

Professor Sun attaches great importance to foster brilliant medical scientists for the country. As a doctor, section chief and college teacher, he has trained a number of high-achieving scientists. His biggest wish is to 'achieve more in research and nurture more talents'. To this end, he was devoted to and strict with young doctors and postgraduates, treating them with sincerity and teaching them hands-on regardless of their age. He aimed not only to enhance their clinical capability, but also to discover, respect and encourage them to use their fortes. He is always ready to detect ideas for research in clinical problems and ask his students to turn their attention to a higher level and solve the clinical difficulties that more badly need to be overcome. Thanks to his guidance, one group after another of young and middle-aged professionals stood out.

Zhang Hongjia, a former doctoral candidate who graduated in 2003, is now a chief physician and leader of clinical affairs. As the head of the research section of Anzhen Hospital, he continues to study dissecting aortic aneurysm. Doctor Lin Changyan is now the director of Biomedical Engineering Research Office and in charge of Beijing New Star of Science and Technology Project. Doctor Qu Zheng is now the director of the hospital's lab; the findings of his experiments on animals for the treatment of coronary heart disease with laser and their clinical application have been included in Cardiac Surgery by Zhu Xiaodong; he is also in charge of the New Star project. Doctor Liu Yuyong is acclaimed by patients for his devotion to research and clinical affairs. Doctor Xie Jinsheng is making an in-depth research into the gene and treatment of Marfan syndrome. Doctor Hou Xiaotong is a chief physician at the perfusion section and deputy director of Anzhen Hospital's cardiopulmonary bypass section. Postdoctoral student Jiang Chaoguang is now the head of the research section of the General Hospital of PLA. Doctor Yang Chuanrui is the director and mainstay of the Heart Research Center of Friendship Hospital.

Sun teaches the spirit of medicine by precept and example. In his opinion, the job of a medical teacher is a sacred one with grave responsibility. Imparting medical knowledge is only part of it. As a doctor and a teacher, he thinks it more important to cultivate in his students virtue and work ethics, driving home the essence of the oath they have taken--'I assume reasonability for the health of my patients, who have entrusted me with their lives'.

He frequently says to his students seriously, "What does morality mean to a surgeon? It should be understood in this way: as long as you can cure the patient, you should preserve as many of his healthy organs and tissues as possible and refrain from making any unnecessary excision. You should operate under the guidance of experienced doctors to ensure the safety of the patient and learn from the process. Never operate when you are inexperienced and uncertain, because the scalpel in your hand may affect a person's life and the happiness of a family. At a critical moment, you should have the courage to share the risk of surgery with your patient. Before operation, you should make a full estimation, analysis and judgment of the pros and cons of surgery and conservative treatment to decide if it's necessary to operate. You should care for and guide the patient in his life and health before and after surgery and improve the quality of his post-surgery life as much as possible. Regard the gratitude of your patients as the drive for you to work hard, improve your surgical skills, and better preserve the health of mankind. A real doctor needs to have the courage to take risks for his patients."

All his postgraduates hold him in veneration. In their words, "President Sun not only teaches us to learn, but also teaches us how to conduct ourselves and do our work."

为首都医科大学学生授课
Lecturing students at
Capital Medical University

1990年5月首都医科大学临床医学六系毕业合影

Group photo of the students graduating from Department Six (Clinical Medicine) of the Capital University of Medical Sciences in May 1990

教学相长 弦歌不辍

A lasting teaching career

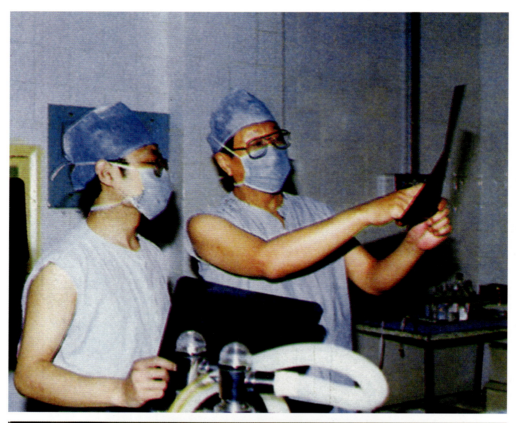

术前为学生讲解X光片
Explaining X-ray films for students before surgery

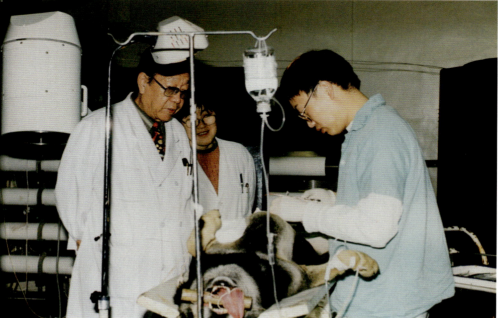

指导学生做动物实验
Supervising students experimenting on animals

为研究生授课
Lecturing postgraduates

参加学位授予仪式

At a degree ceremony

与研究生合影
With postgraduates

鼠年春节在家中与学生、同事合影

With students and colleagues during the Spring Festival in the Year of Rat

2008年中华胸心血管外科学会领导春节拜年

A courtesy call paid by leaders of China Society of Thoracic and Cardiovascular Surgery during the Spring Festival of 2008

教学相长 弦歌不辍

A lasting teaching career

2009年7月86岁寿辰与博士、博士后研究生合影

With doctor candidates and postdoctoral students at his 86th birthday in July 2009

73

中 美 冠 心 病 诊 疗 培 训 中 心 首 期

国 学 习 班　1998.11.2-9北京钓鱼台国宾馆

1998年11月中美冠心病诊疗培训中心首期全国学习班合影

The first national workshop at the Sino-American Training Center for the Diagnosis and Treatment of Coronary Heart Disease in November 1998

教学相长 弦歌不辍

A lasting teaching career

2009年9月获"吴阶
平桃李奖"

Receiving Wu Jieping
Award for Teachers in
September 2009

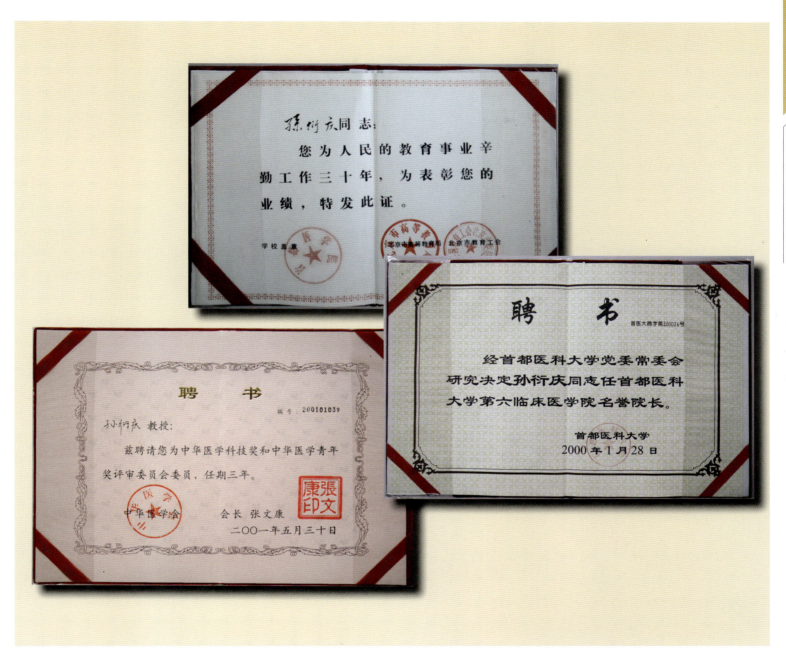

致力于医学教育事业
Dedication to medical education

飞廉作意恣撝翥
万壑千岩气象雄
独鹤梦中摇夜月
七经微外寄秋鞍
石坛蹑墨支笻里
天竺斋余隐几中

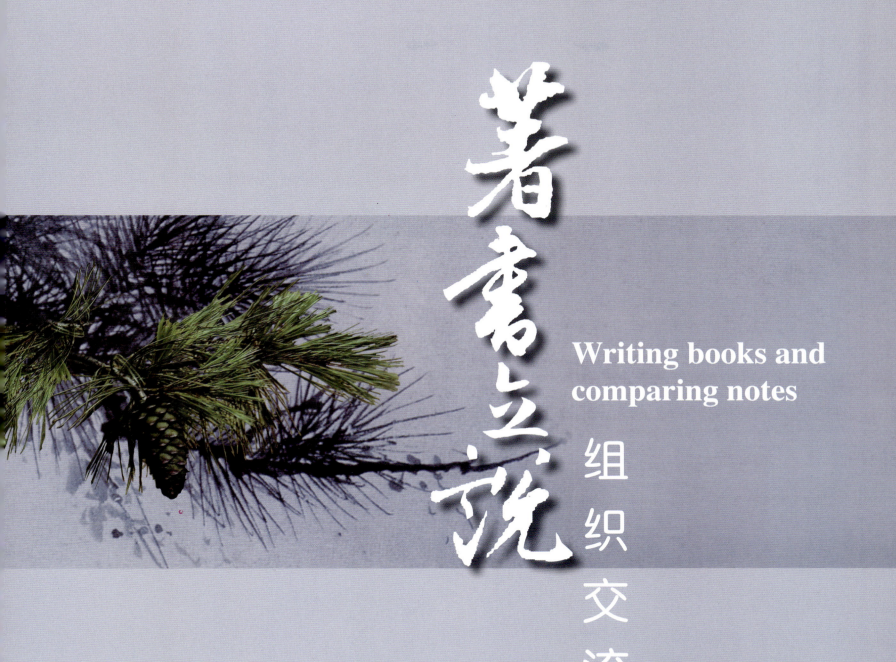

著書立说

组织交流

Writing books and
comparing notes

# 五、著书立说  组织交流

从20世纪50年代开始，孙衍庆就致力于关于肝硬变引起门脉高压症外科治疗的系统研究，并于60年代提出"根据门脉高压中门脉系统和下腔血液动力学压力指数的不同而设计了限制性门腔静脉侧侧分流术"。80年代，他通过动物实验与临床研究，设计研制了专用三翼钳和剪刀等器械，证实了完全分流是由于吻合口过大引起肝性脑病等，在国内首次提出并创造了根据血液动力学指标计算最佳吻合口的公式。此项工作早于美国22年，荣获国家科技进步二等奖，根据这一成果主编的《门静脉高压症的外科治疗研究》一书，全面论述了我国的治疗现状。

1982年，孙衍庆教授首先在国内报告主动脉夹层动脉瘤外科治疗的成功。由于他对该手术过程中心脑肺脏器的保护进行了较广泛的系统研究与临床应用，使手术死亡率及术后生存率均达到世界先进水平。他对该病病因及发病机制的研究首次证明，我国90%以上病因为主动脉中层囊性坏死，而国外为动脉硬化；我国发病年龄较欧美早10~20岁。这为我国开展对此疾病的预防提供了重要理论依据，荣获国家科技进步二等奖。

关于马凡氏综合征心脏大血管病变外科治疗是孙衍庆教授又一颇有特色的系统研究。自1985年他在国内首次采用Bentall手术获得成功并填补了国内此项空白以来，针对该疾病的诊断开展了分子生物学研究，即马凡综合征基因研究、临床表型与基因表达的相关性研究、基因诊断的临床应用以及预测预防等。针对手术治疗开展了深低温停循环经上腔静脉逆行灌注脑保护、经冠状静脉窦持续冷—温血灌注心肌保护等研究。针对围术期并发症制定了手术技术与术后处理的规范。其研究成果达国际先进水平，是我国心脏外科发展水平的标志，有力地推动了我国心血管外科的发展，荣获国家科技进步二等奖。

1974年，孙衍庆开始担任《国外医学外科学分册》的总编辑，随后兼任过《健康咨询报》和《北京生物医学工程杂志》的总编辑。此外孙衍庆教授还曾被选为4个全国性学会的理事长或副理事长、北京市科协常务理事、名誉委员。

1985—1992年，他当选为中华医学会胸心血管外科学会第一、第二届副主任委员，协助苏鸿熙主任委员，为推动我国胸心血管外科的发展做了大量工作。在创办学会代表性杂志《胸心血管外科杂志》（后改为《中华胸心血管外科杂志》）期间，孙衍庆做出了突出贡献。杂志创刊后，他先后担任副总编、总编辑工作。孙衍庆教授在任学会第三届主任委员的4年间，继承和发扬"勤俭办会、以会养会"的优良传统与作风，积极开展学术交流活动，共召开或联合召开全国性和国际性的学术会议12次。

孙衍庆没有出国留过学，是地地道道的"国产"医学专家；但他始终认为，科学技术是没有国界的。20世纪80年代以来，国内交流、出国访问和国际交流多了，孙衍庆不放过任何学习机会，他虚心采纳众家之长，上至理论学说，小到手术技巧，都经过消化吸收，变成自己的本领。从60年代至今，他多次到日本、新加坡、几内亚、美国、前苏联、法国、意大利、德国、阿根廷等30多个国家访问、考察、手术和学术交流，以丰富提高自己。"科学技术是没有国界的，我接触过日、德、英、美、俄等不同国家的医学家，以及国内不同学派的医学家，他们的思路、手术风格、临床医疗特点各异，可以说是各有所长、各有千秋。我的有些知识和手术技巧就是从他们那里学来的，这样做使我的知识丰富起来，也少走了很多弯路。"他去阿根廷意大利医院学习低架猪生物瓣膜制作工艺，回国后组织研制小组完成了"适当低架生物心瓣膜"的制作，并在临床应用50例取得满意效果。

# V. Writing books and comparing notes

From 1950s, Sun Yanqing began his research into the surgical treatment of portal hypertension caused by hepatic cirrhosis. In the 1960s, he devised restrictive portacaval shunt according to the difference in the pressure indices of the portal system and the vena hemodynamics in portal hypertension. In the 1980s, after experiments on animals and clinical research, he developed the three-wing clamp and the specialized scissors, proved that the reason for complete shunt is hepatic encephalopathy caused by the excessive size of the stoma, and was the first in China to put forward the formula for calculating optimal stoma size according to hemodynamic indices, which was not discovered in the United States until 22 years later. He received a second-class National Award for Progress in Science and Technology for that formula. Based on it, he published Surgical Treatment of Portal Hypertension as a comprehensive description of the status quo of the treatment of the condition in China.

In 1982, Professor Sun became the first in China to report the success of the surgical treatment of aortic dissecting aneurysm. His extensive and systematic study and clinical application of the protection of the heart, the brain and the lungs during the surgery helped to lower the rate of death from surgery and increase the rate of survival after surgery to an advanced world level. His research into the causes and mechanism of the disease proved for the first time that over 90% of the cases in China are caused by cystic medial necrosis of aorta whereas the primary cause abroad is arteriosclerosis, and that those affected with the disease are ten to twenty years younger than their counterparts in Europe and America. He received a second-class National Award for Progress in Science and Technology for his findings, which have provided an important theoretical basis for the prevention of the disease in China.

The surgical treatment of cardiovascular conditions due to the Marfan syndrome is yet another finding of his special systematic research. In 1985, he became the first in China to successfully perform the Bentall surgery. Since then, he has conducted molecular biological research into the diagnosis of the condition, including genetic research into the Marfan syndrome, correlational research of clinical phenotype and gene expression, the clinical application of genetic diagnosis, and prediction and prevention of the condition. For surgical treatment, he researched retrograde cerebral perfusion via superior vena cava in deep hypothermic circulatory arrest and myocardial protection by cold and warm blood perfusion via coronary sinus. He drew up the standard for surgical technique and post-surgery treatment for perioperative complications. His findings, which have achieved the advanced world level and won him a second-class National Award for Progress in Science and Technology, mark the cutting edge of cardiac surgery in China and provide a powerful impetus to the development of cardiovascular surgery in the country.

In 1974, he was appointed editor-in-chief of the volume on surgery in Medicine in Foreign Countries. Later he was concurrently the editor-in-chief of the newspaper Health Advice and Beijing Biomedical Engineering Journal. Besides, he was elected president or vice-president of the councils of four national academic societies, an executive member of the council and an honorary member of Beijing Science Association.

From 1985 to 1992, he was elected vice chairman of the first and second committee of the thoracic and cardiovascular surgery branch of the Chinese Medical Association. As an assistant to Chairman Su Hongxi, he did much to improve thoracic and cardiovascular surgery in China. He made prominent contribution to the founding of the society's primary journal, The Journal of Thoracic and Cardiovascular Surgery (later renamed China Journal of Thoracic and Cardiovascular Surgery). Ever since the journal came into being, he has been at first vice editor-in-chief and then editor-in-chief. During his four-year term as chairman of the third committee of the society, he carried on its tradition, organizing events for comparing notes and convening twelve national and international academic conferences.

Though he has never studied abroad, Sun always believe that science and technology have no borders. Domestic and international exchange and visits to foreign countries brought about a boom. Sun let no opportunity to learn slip by, incorporating an extensive range of theories and skills into his capability. Since the 1960s, he has been to over thirty countries, including Japan, Singapore, Guinea, America, forme soviet Union, France, Italy, Germany and Argentina, for observation, surgery and academic exchange. 'Science and technology have no borders. I have met medical scientists from different countries, such as Japan, Germany, Britain, America and Russia and those of different schools in China. They differ widely in ways of thinking, surgical style and clinical treatment, and I've acquired some of my knowledge and skills from them. By doing so, I enriched my learning and avoided many detours.'

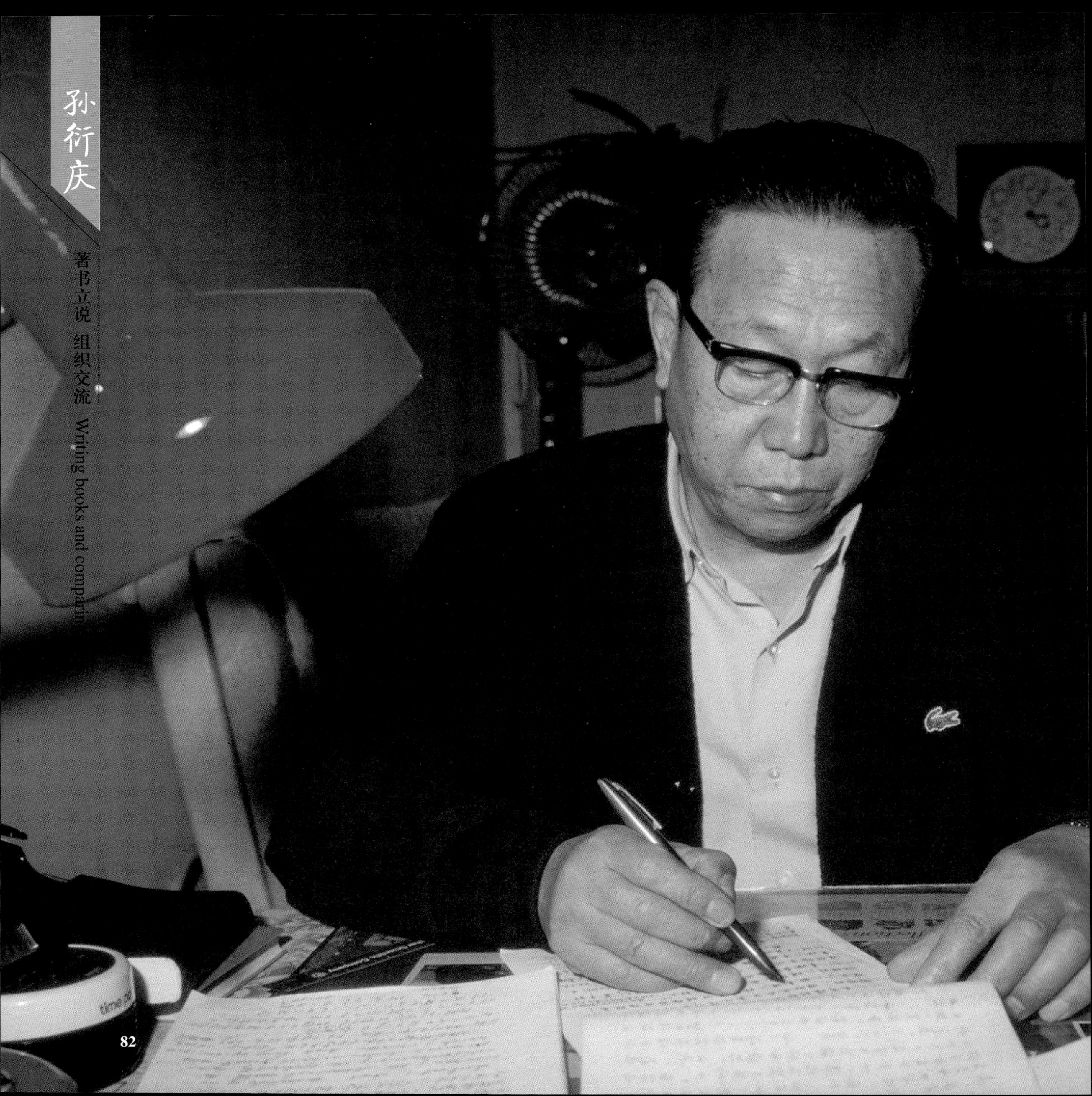

孙衍庆

著书立说　组织交流

Writing books and comparing notes

伏案整理论文
Sorting out academic
papers at his desk

著述等身

A prolific writer

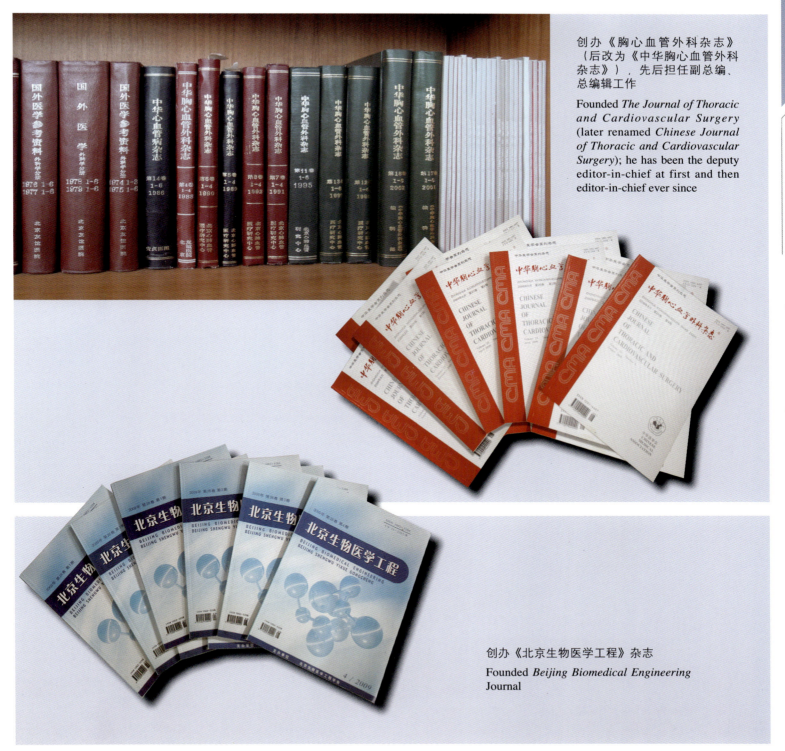

创办《胸心血管外科杂志》（后改为《中华胸心血管外科杂志》），先后担任副总编、总编辑工作

Founded *The Journal of Thoracic and Cardiovascular Surgery* (later renamed *Chinese Journal of Thoracic and Cardiovascular Surgery*); he has been the deputy editor-in-chief at first and then editor-in-chief ever since

创办《北京生物医学工程》杂志

Founded *Beijing Biomedical Engineering Journal*

感谢您在创建和发展北京市
科学技术协会及其所属团体事业中
所做出的贡献

北京市科学技术协会主席 陈方舟

孙衍庆 教授留念

泱泱医术　袭袭宗师

中华外科杂志第九届编辑委员会　敬赠
中华外科杂志编辑部
一九九五年九月

备受肯定

Fully acknowledged
for his work

任友谊医院外科主任时接待外宾

Receiving foreign visitors as head of the Surgical
Department of Friendship Hospital

20世纪80年代初在友谊医院接待美国外宾

Receiving American visitors at Friendship Hospital in the early 1980s

在中苏友谊医院时的苏联专家纳格尼别达夫妇回国30年后来信寄来的照片。

The photo enclosed in the letter sent by former Soviet experts Nagnibeda and his wife 30 years after they left Sino-Soviet Friendship Hospital and returned to Russia

纳格尼别达曾说："临床医生不仅要治好病，还要教会人们预防疾病；最重要的是不能只做外科技匠，一定要做医学研究，做推动医学科学进步与发展的医学科学家。"这对孙衍庆影响至深。

Nagnibeda said, "A clinical doctor must not only cure diseases but also teach people to prevent them. Most importantly, he must not be nothing more than a surgical craftsman; instead, he must do medical research and be a medical scientist contributing to the progress of medical science."

与纳格尼别达夫妇合影
With the Nagnibedas

20世纪80年代初赴阿根廷
布宜诺斯艾利斯考察

In Buenos Aires, Argentina in
the early 1980s

在阿根廷与外国专家交流

Comparing notes with foreign
experts in Argentina

在友谊医院与瑞典学生代表团合影

With a delegation of Swedish students at Friendship Hospital

Simposio Internazionale su
"Le arteriopatie ostruttive
degli arti inferiori nei giovani"

1982年在罗马参加学术会议并作学术报告

Attending an academic conference and giving an
academic speech there in Rome in 1982

Simposio Internazionale su
"Le arteriopatie ostruttive
degli arti inferiori nei giovani"

Roma, 20-22 Maggio 1982

著书立说 组织交流

Writing books and comparing notes

访问苏联期间参观医院

Visit to a hospital during
his stay in the Soviet Union

20世纪80年代在列宁格勒
为烈士墓献花

Presenting flowers to
a grave of martyrs in
Leningrad in the 1980s

Professor Sun — The day you + your colleagues spent with me in Washington were one of the most enjoyable I've ever had —
John Brzezinski Dec. 3, '87

1979年在美国考察

In America in 1979

任北京市卫生局局长期间访问坦桑尼亚

Visiting Tanzania as head of the Beijing Public Health Bureau

任北京市卫生局局长时赴非洲坦桑尼亚慰问医疗队

Extending regards to the medical team during his visit to Tanzania as head of the Beijing Public Health Bureau

在坦桑尼亚与当地官
员合影

With local officials in
Tanzania

任北京市卫生局局长
期间接待外宾

Receiving foreign
visitors as head of the
Beijing Public Health
Bureau

著书立说 组织交流

Writing books and comparing notes

任北京市卫生局局长
期间访问日本并讲课

Visiting Japan and
lecturing there as head
of the Beijing Public
Health Bureau

接受日本华侨捐赠的血
液透析设备

Receiving a hemodialysis
device from Chinese
immigrants in Japan

与日本东京都友好代表团合影
With the Friendship Delegation
of Tokyo Metropolitan

1988年参加中日难治性胰腺
疾病学术交流会

Sino-Japanese Academic
Seminar on Difficult Pancreas
Diseases in 1988

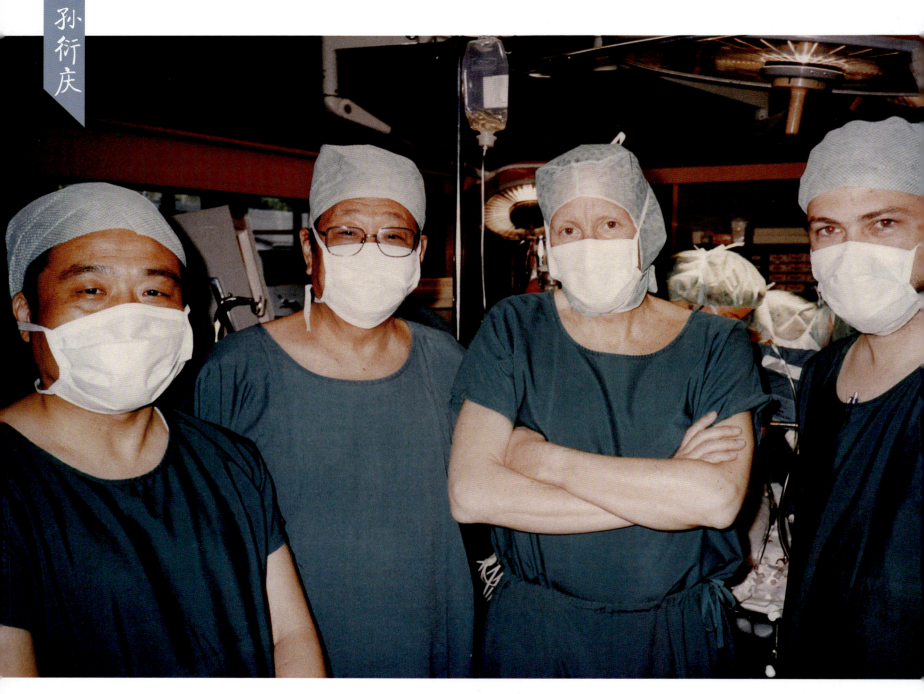

1990年4月在瑞士访问时与瑞士同行合影

With Swedish colleagues during his visit to Sweden in April 1990

与外交部长李肇星及华
裔心脏内科专家郑宗鄂
合影

With Foreign Minister Li
Zhaoxing and Chinese
American cardiology
expert Zheng Zong'e

在安贞医院接待外宾

Receiving foreign visitors
at Anzhen Hospital

第四届中国国际胸心外科学术会议上孙衍庆教授与美国心外专家Lilleihi在一起

With American cardiac surgery expert Dr. Lilleihi at the Fourth China International Academic Conference on Cardio-thoracic Surgery

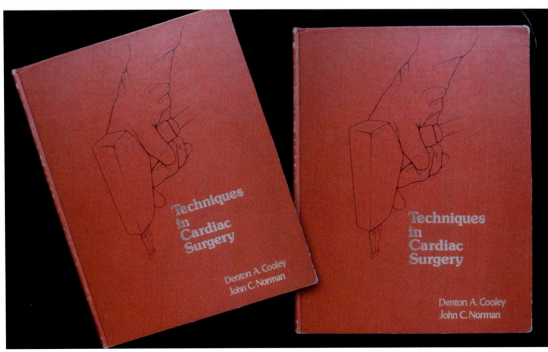

March 2, 1979

To Dr. Y. C. Sun

With warmest regards and a sincere welcome to our first surgical visitor from the People's Republic of China.

Denton A. Cooley M.D.

**Techniques in Cardiac Surgery**

Denton A. Cooley, M.D.
Surgeon-in-chief

John C. Norman, M.D.
Attending Surgeon

Foreword by Lord Brock

1979年访问美国德克萨斯州心脏病研究所世界著名心脏外科专家D.A.库力教授签名赠书：热烈欢迎第一位来自人民中国的访问学者

Receiving a book autographed by world-famous cardiac surgery expert Professor D. A. Kulick during his visit to Texas Heart Institute in 1979; he was given a warm welcome as the first visiting scholar from the People's Republic of China

全国首届胸心血管外科
学术会议主席团合影

The presidium of the
First National Academic
Conference on Thoracic
and Cardiovascular
Surgery

1983年中华医学会第十
届外科委员会全体合影

The entire 10th Surgery
Committee of Chinese
Medical Association in
1983

1983年中华医学会北京分会第十二届理事会理事合影

Members of the 12th Council of the Beijing Branch of Chinese Medical Association in 1983

1985年中华医学会北京分会第十三届理事会理事合影

Members of the 13th council of the Beijing Branch of Chinese Medical Association in 1985

2006年春节拜访苏鸿熙教授

Visiting professor Su Hongxi during the Spring Festival in 2006

2004年第四、第五届胸心外科学会主任委员交接时与朱晓东教授合影

With professor Zhu Xiaodong at the handover between the chairpersons of the 4th and 5th Cardiac Surgery Society in 2004

2001年9月在首届名
医论坛上作报告

Giving a speech at
the First Forum of
Eminent Doctors in
September 2001

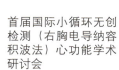

首届国际小循环无创
检测（右胸电导纳容
积波法）心功能学术
研讨会

The First International
Academic Seminar
on Small-cycle Non-
invasive Detection of
Cardiac Function (with
Right-chest Sodium
Conductance Volume
Wave)

**110**

2005年5月中华医学基金会常务理事合影

Executive members of the council of China Medical Association in May 2005

与钱信忠、白介夫、朱宗涵等领导合影

With Qian Xinzhong, Bai Jiefu, Zhu Zonghan and other leaders

著书立说 组织交流

Writing books and comparing notes

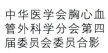

中华医学会胸心血
管外科学分会第四
届委员会委员合影

Members of the
4th Committee of
the Thoracic and
Cardiovascular
Surgery Branch
of China Medical
Association

1995年参加全国冠状动脉外
科专题研讨会

At the National Symposium on
Coronary Surgery in 1995

参加人工心脏瓣膜质量标准
审定会

At the Meeting for Approving
the Criteria of the Quality of
Artificial Heart Valves

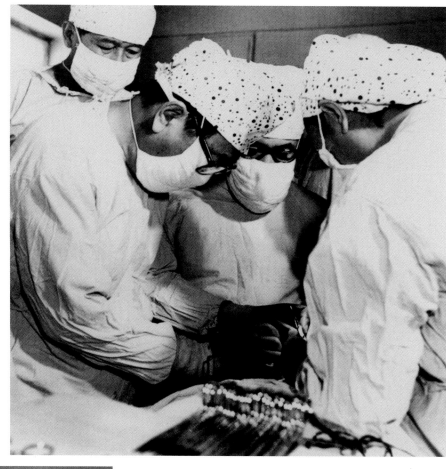

赴新疆协助开展手术

Helping conduct
surgery in Xinjiang

左起苏鸿熙教授、孙衍庆教授、黄国俊教授在学术交流

Prof. Su Hongxi, Prof. Sun Yanqing and Prof. Huang Guojun (from left to right) comparing notes

1985年上海兰锡纯教授（中）丁之祥教授（左一）来院参观，与吴英恺院长（左二）、孙衍庆院长（右二）和王慧玲主任合影

In 1985, Prof. Lan Xichun (in the middle) and Prof. Ding Zhixiang (first from the left) from Shanghai visited the hospital and had this photo taken with President Wu Yingkai (second from the left), President Sun Yanqing (second from the right) and Director Wang Huiling

泽陂有微草

能花复能实

碧叶喜翻风

红英宜照日

敷居玉池上

托根庭非尖

励精图治 谋利于民

Vigorous efforts
for the benefit of
the people

## 六、励精图治　谋利于民

1983—1987年，孙衍庆担任北京市卫生局局长。之前担任友谊医院副院长的孙衍庆更倾向于继续从事自己的业务工作，时任市委第一书记的段君毅亲自找孙衍庆谈心，副市长白介夫又"三顾茅庐"。白介夫副市长语重心长，"业务固然重要，但抓好首都全面的卫生工作更有意义"。

对于孙衍庆而言，卫生局长不仅仅是一个职位，更意味着厚重的责任和辛劳。他热爱手术台、热爱病人；同时，他也牢记"顾大局、谋大利"的信念。于是从专家到局长，他以同样认真的态度，对北京市的医疗卫生行政管理工作殚精竭虑，付出了极大的心血。

20世纪80年代任卫生局领导期间，在北京市委、市政府的领导下，孙衍庆立志改革，在解决住院难的问题、加强基层医院建设、加强儿童与老年疾病预防治疗，以及加强以预防为主等方面做出了功不可灭的业绩。他积极支持并参与成立北京市心肺血管疾病医疗研究中心——安贞医院。他提出的《改革公费医疗与劳保医疗的设想》曾发表于1991年中国医院管理杂志，与当今全社会医疗公费改革的思维潮流相一致，深具现实意义。

街道医院和区县医院房屋简陋、设备陈旧和技术水平低的问题，长期没有引起重视。孙衍庆在时任卫生部长崔月犁的大力支持下，改建了丰盛医院、德外医院和崇文区中医医院等小医院，由大医院与小医院挂钩，提高了小医院的技术水平。他主持成立卫生（护士）学校，大力培养卫生专业人才；同时，他极力促成解放军医院向民众开放，缓解了百姓看病难、住院难的重大问题。

孙衍庆特别注意农村医疗工作，深入基层帮助10个郊区县改建扩建了县医院，并建立顺义卫生学校，定点培养农村医师，为发展农村医疗工作培养了大批人才。

他致力于普及健康知识，创办了《健康咨询报》，并亲自任社长兼主编，撰写科普文章，使老百姓容易接受并能学以致用，"防病于未然"，而真正受益。

20世纪80年代初，中国没有自己的康复中心，很多人因为没有康复的机会而丧失了恢复健康的希望。孙衍庆在任北京市卫生局局长期间，大力协助中国残疾人联合会建立中国的康复中心，在医疗方面给予了大量人力物力的支持，推动了中国康复事业的发展，也为中国的残疾人事业做出了突出的贡献。

在担任北京市卫生局局长期间，孙衍庆经常回医院做一些疑难手术，从未放下过手术刀。他在卫生局长和医学专家之间做出平衡，以超乎寻常的毅力，在短短4年里为提高北京市的医疗卫生工作水平做出了突出贡献。

现在孙衍庆教授已逾86岁高龄。他依然坚持定时出专家门诊，指导疑难手术，回答病人的咨询；依然伏案编书审稿，积极参加学术交流和研究生论文答辩，关心医学科学前沿的发展。"莫道桑榆晚，为霞尚满天"，作为中国胸心血管外科一代宗师，孙衍庆教授坚持振兴祖国、强健民族的信念，依旧不知疲倦地在胸心血管外科领域默默耕耘。

# VI. Vigorous efforts for the benefit of the people

From 1983 to 1987, Sun Yanqing was the head of the Public Health Bureau of Beijing. Before that, as the vice president of Friendship Hospital, he would like more to continue his professional career. Duan Junyi, the first party secretary of Beijing at the time, talked to him in person. Vice Mayor Bai Jiefu paid him several visits, saying earnestly, "Your professional career is important, but it is more important to bring about an overall improvement of public health in the capital."

For Sun, the head of the Public Health Bureau was more than an office, for it meant a heavy responsibility and toil. He loved the operating table and patients, but he was also aware of the overall interest and the greater good. Because of that, as head of the bureau, he spared no effort to improve the administration of health care in Beijing.

In the 1980s, as the head of the Public Health Bureau under the leadership of the party committee and municipal government of Beijing, Sun was resolved to implement reform, leaving indelible marks on facilitating hospitalization, improving grass-roots hospitals, the prevention and treatment of pediatric and geriatic diseases, and giving priority to prevention. He actively supported and participated in the founding of Anzhen Hospital, which is also Beijing Research Center of Heart and Lung Vessel Diseases. His *Tentative Plan of Reforming Free Medical Service at State Expense and Medical Service under Labor Insurance*, published in China Journal of Hospital Administration in 1991, remains meaningful because of its consistency with today's call for reforming free medical care.

The shabby houses, outdated equipment and backward technical level of community, district and county hospitals had been ignored for a long time . Under the vigorous support of the then Minister of Health Cui Yueli, Sun rebuilt small hospitals such as Fengsheng Hospital, Dewai Hospital and the Hospital of Traditional Chinese Medicine of Chongwen District. He improved the technical level of small hospitals by linking them with large ones. He founded medical (nurse) schools to train professional medical workers. Meanwhile, he successfully made PLA hospitals accessible to civilians, making it easier for them to obtain medical service and get hospitalized.

Sun set great store by health care in rural areas. He went down to the grass-roots and helped ten suburban districts and counties rebuild or expand their hospitals. He founded Shunyi Medical School, which has trained a large number of country doctors.

To popularize knowledge about health, he founded the newspaper Health Advice, acting as the president and editor-in-chief and writing pop science articles for common people to learn to prevent diseases.

In the 1980s, when China had no rehabilitation centers, many were denied the chance of recovery. When in office, Sun vigorously helped the Association of the Disabled found rehabilitation centers. His supply of large quantities human and material resources of health care helped to develop rehabilitation services and contributed prominently to the care of the disabled in China.

When in office, instead of bidding farewell to the scalpel, Sun frequently returned to the hospital to perform difficult operations. He struck a balance between his roles as head of the bureau and a medical specialist. With extraordinary willpower, he did an outstanding job in improving health care in Beijing within the short period of four years.

Professor Sun Yanqing is now 86 years old. Despite his age, he still receives outpatients on a regular basis, supervise difficult operations, and answer patients' questions. He continues to write books, review drafts, takes an active part in academic exchange and postgraduates' oral defense of their theses, and keep abreast of the latest developments in medical sciences. 'One is never too old to learn.' As a master of thoracic and cardiovascular surgery, Professor Sun adheres to his faith in the reinvigoration of the country and the nation and continues his unflagging research in his field.

励精图治 谋利于民 *Vigorous efforts for the benefit of the people*

参加政协分组讨论会
At a group discussion
of the CPPCC

励精图治 谋利于民 Vigorous efforts for the benefit of the people

参加政协讨论

At a discussion organized by the CPPCC

**123**

1993年全国政协会议上与国家医药管理局局
长齐谋甲合影

With Qi Moujia, head of the State Pharmaceutical
Administration at the CPPCC National
Conference in 1993

励精图治 谋利于民

*Vigorous efforts for the benefit of the people*

全国政协第七、第八届
文教卫生委员会委员

Members of the 7th
and 8th Committee of
Culture, Education and
Health of the National
CPPCC

**125**

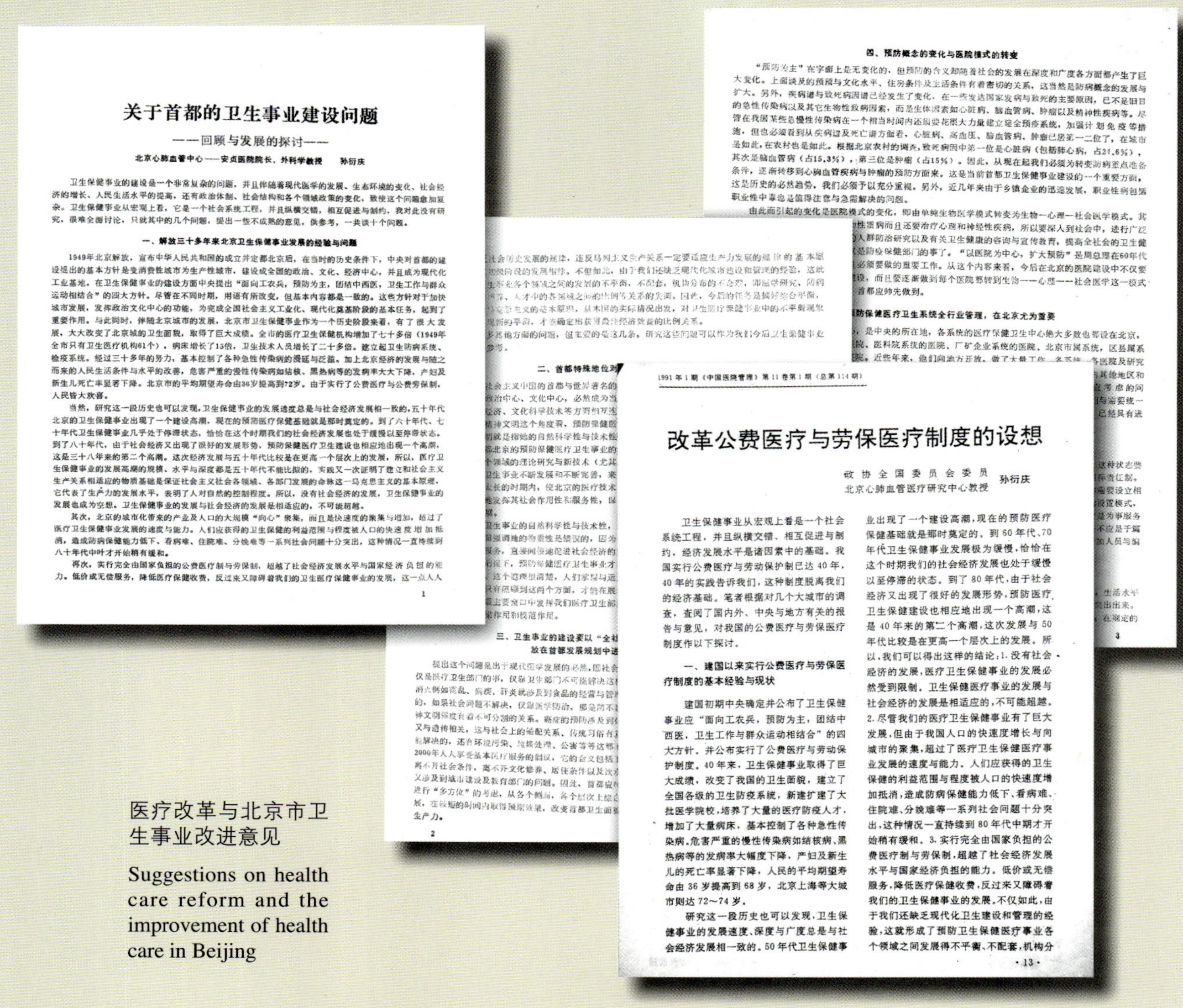

# 关于首都的卫生事业建设问题

——回顾与发展的探讨——

北京心肺血管中心——安贞医院院长、外科学教授　孙衍庆

卫生保健事业的建设是一个非常复杂的问题，并且伴随着现代医学的发展、生态环境的变化、社会经济的增长、人民生活水平的提高，还有政治体制、社会结构和各个领域政策的变化，致使这个问题愈加复杂。卫生保健事业从宏观上看，它是一个社会系统工程，并且纵横交错，相互促进与制约，我对此没有研究，很难全面讨论，只就其中的几个问题，提出一些不成熟的意见，供参考，一共谈十个问题。

一、解放三十多年来北京卫生保健事业发展的经验与问题

1949年北京解放，宣布中华人民共和国的成立并定都北京后，在当时的历史条件下，中央对首都的建设提出的基本方针是变消费性城市为生产性城市，建设成全国的政治、文化、经济中心，并且成为现代化工业基地。在卫生保健事业的建设方面中央提出“面向工农兵，预防为主，团结中西医，卫生工作与群众运动相结合”的四大方针。尽管在不同时期，用语有所改变，但基本内容都是一致的。这些方针对于加快城市发展，发挥政治文化中心的功能，为完成全国社会主义工业化、现代化奠基阶段的基本任务，起到了重要作用。与此同时，伴随北京城市的发展，北京市卫生保健事业作为一个历史阶段来看，有了很大发展，大大改变了北京城的卫生面貌，取得了巨大成绩。全市的医疗卫生保健机构增加了七十多倍（1949年全市只有卫生医疗机构61个），病床增长了15倍，卫生技术人员增长了二十多倍。建立起卫生防病系统、检疫系统。经过三十多年的努力，基本控制了各种急性传染病的漫延与泛滥。加上北京经济的发展与随之而来的人民生活条件与水平的改善，危害严重的慢性传染病如结核、黑热病等的发病率大大下降，产妇及新生儿死亡率显著下降。北京市的平均期望寿命由36岁提高到72岁。由于实行了公费医疗与公费劳保制，人民皆大欢喜。

当然，研究这一段历史也可以发现，卫生保健事业的发展速度总是与社会经济发展相一致的，五十年代北京的卫生保健事业出现了一个建设高潮，现在的预防医疗保健基础就是那时奠定的。到了六十年代、七十年代卫生保健事业几乎处于停滞状态，恰恰在这个时期我们的社会经济发展也处于缓慢以至停滞状态。到了八十年代，由于社会经济又出现了很好的发展形势，预防保健医疗卫生建设也相应地出现一个高潮，这是三十八年来的第二个高潮。这次经济发展与五十年代比较是在更高一个层次上的发展，所以，医疗卫生保健事业的发展高潮的规模、水平与深度都是五十年代不能比拟的，实践又一次证明了建立和社会主义生产关系相适应的物质基础是保证社会主义社会各领域、各部门发展的命脉这一马克思主义的基本原理，它代表了生产力的发展水平，表明了人对自然的控制程度。所以，没有社会经济的发展，卫生保健事业的发展也成为空想。卫生保健事业的发展与社会经济的发展是相适应的，不可能超越。

其次，北京的城市化带来的产业及人口的大规模“向心”聚集，而且是快速度的聚集与增加，超过了医疗卫生保健事业发展的速度与能力。人们应获得的卫生保健的利益范围与程度被人口的快速度增加抵消，造成防病保健能力低下、看病难、住院难、分娩难等一系列社会问题十分突出，这种情况一直持续到八十年代中叶才开始稍有缓和。

再次，实行完全由国家负担的公费医疗制与劳保制，超越了社会经济发展水平与国家经济负担的能力。低价或无偿服务，降低医疗保健收费，反过来又障碍着我们的卫生医疗保健事业的发展，这一点人人

1

四、预防概念的变化与医院模式的转变

“预防为主”在字面上是无变化的，但预防的含义却随着社会的发展在深度和广度各方面都产生了巨大变化。上面谈及的预预与文化水平、住房条件及生活条件有着密切的关系，这当然是防病概念的发展与扩大。另外，疾病谱与致死病因谱已经发生了变化，在一些发达国家发病与致死的主要原因，已不是旧日的急性传染病以及其它生物性致病因素，而是生体因素如心脏病、脑血管病、肿瘤以及精神性疾病等。尽管在我国某些急慢性传染病在一个相当时间内还须要花很大力量建立建全预疫系统，加强计划免疫等措施，但也必须看到从疾病谱及死亡谱方面看，心脏病、高血压、脑血管病、肿瘤已居第一二位了，在城市是如此，在农村也是如此。根据北京农村的调查，致死病因中第一位是心脏病（包括肺心病，占21.6%），其次是脑血管病（占15.3%），第三位是肿瘤（占15%）。因此，从现在起我们必须为转变防病重点准备条件，逐渐转移到心胸血管疾病与肿瘤的预防方面来。这是当前首都卫生保健事业建设的一个重要方面，这是历史的必然趋势，我们必须予以充分重视。另外，近几年来由于乡镇企业的迅速发展，职业性病包括职业性中毒也是值得注意与急需解决的问题。

1991 年 1 期（中国医院管理）第 11 卷第 1 期（总第 114 期）

# 改革公费医疗与劳保医疗制度的设想

政协全国委员会委员
北京心肺血管医疗研究中心教授　孙衍庆

卫生保健事业从宏观上看是一个社会系统工程，并且纵横交错、相互促进与制约，经济发展水平是诸因素中的基础。我国实行公费医疗与劳动保护制已达 40 年，40 年的实践告诉我们，这种制度脱离我们的经济基础。笔者根据对几个大城市的调查，查阅了国内外、中央与地方有关的报告与意见，对我国的公费医疗与劳保医疗制度作以下探讨。

一、建国以来实行公费医疗与劳保医疗制度的基本经验与现状

建国初期中央确定并公布了卫生保健事业应“面向工农兵，预防为主，团结中西医，卫生工作与群众运动相结合”的四大方针。并公布实行了公费医疗与劳动保护制度。40 年来，卫生保健事业取得了巨大成绩，改变了我国的卫生面貌，建立了全国各级的卫生防疫系统，新建扩建了大批医学院校，培养了大量的医疗防疫人才，增加了大量病床，基本控制了各种急性传染病。危害严重的慢性传染病如结核病、黑热病等的发病率大幅度下降，产妇及新生儿的死亡率显著下降，人民的平均期望寿命由 36 岁提高到 68 岁，北京上海等大城市则达 72～74 岁。

研究这一段历史也可以发现，卫生保健事业的发展速度、深度与广度总是与社会经济发展相一致的。50 年代卫生保健事业出现了一个建设高潮，现在的预防医疗保健基础就是那时奠定的。到 60 年代、70 年代卫生保健事业发展极为缓慢，恰恰在这个时期我们的社会经济发展也处于缓慢以至停滞的状态。到了 80 年代，由于社会经济又出现了很好的发展形势，预防医疗卫生保健建设也相应地出现一个高潮，这是 40 年来的第二个高潮，这次发展与 50 年代比较是在更高一个层次上的发展。所以，我们可以得出这样的结论：1. 没有社会经济的发展，医疗卫生保健事业的发展必然受到限制。卫生保健医疗事业的发展与社会经济的发展是相适应的，不可能超越。2. 尽管我们的医疗卫生保健事业有了巨大发展，但由于我国人口的快速度增长与向城市的聚集，超过了医疗卫生保健医疗事业发展的速度与能力。人们应获得的卫生保健的利益范围与程度被人口的快速度增加抵消，造成防病保健能力低下、看病难、住院难、分娩难等一系列社会问题十分突出，这种情况一直持续到 80 年代中期才开始稍有缓和。3. 实行完全由国家负担的公费医疗制与劳保制，超越了社会经济发展水平与国家经济负担的能力。低价或无偿服务，降低医疗保健收费，反过来又障碍着我们的卫生保健事业的发展。不仅如此，由于我们还缺乏现代化卫生建设和管理的经验，这就形成了预防卫生保健医疗事业各个领域之间发展得不平衡、不配套，机构分

·13·

医疗改革与北京市卫生事业改进意见

Suggestions on health care reform and the improvement of health care in Beijing

北京市卫生局局长任命书

Letter of appointment of the chief
of Beijing Public Health Bureau

≪ 丰台医院
Fengtai Hospital

≫ 房山卫校
Fangshan Medical School

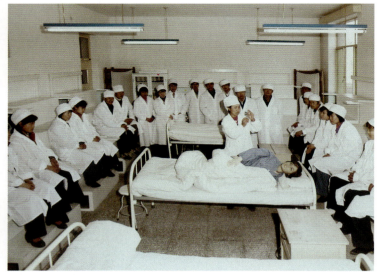

≪ 北京护士学校
Beijing Nurses' School

在任北京市卫生局局长期间，改建、扩建和新建区县和街道医院，扩建急救中心，合理布局医疗网点方便群众就医，建立卫生（护士）学校培养卫生人才

While in office, he rebuilt, expanded and built distrct, county and community hospitals, expanded emergency centers, and introduced a well-designed health care network to make it easier to people to get medical service. He founded medical (nurse) schools to train health care personnel.

≪ 北新桥医院
Beixinqiao Hospital

卫生防疫站
Sanitation and anti-
epidemic station

励精图治 谋利于民

Vigorous efforts for the benefit of the people

2006年3月15日中国残疾人福利基金会送给孙衍庆教授的感谢状

Certificate of gratitude presented to President Sun by China Welfare Fund for the Handicapped on March 15th, 2006

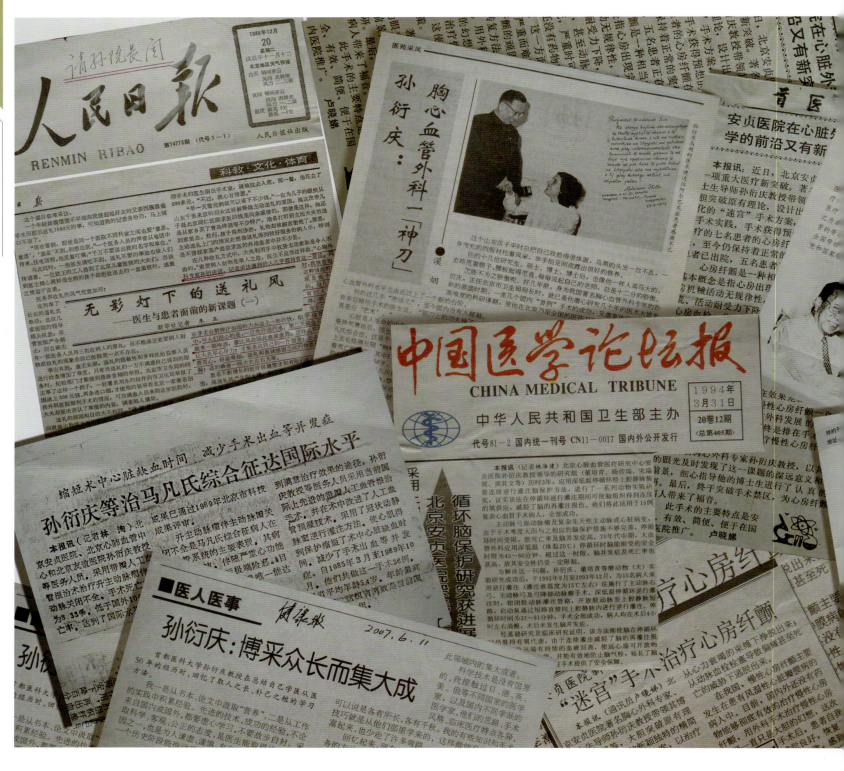

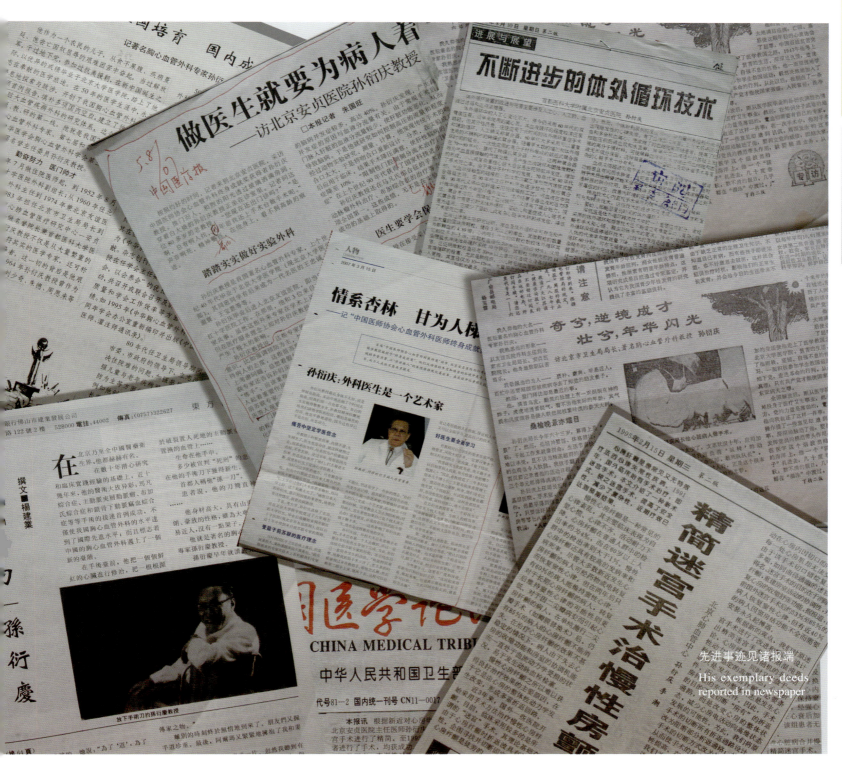

先进事迹见诸报端
His exemplary deeds
reported in newspaper

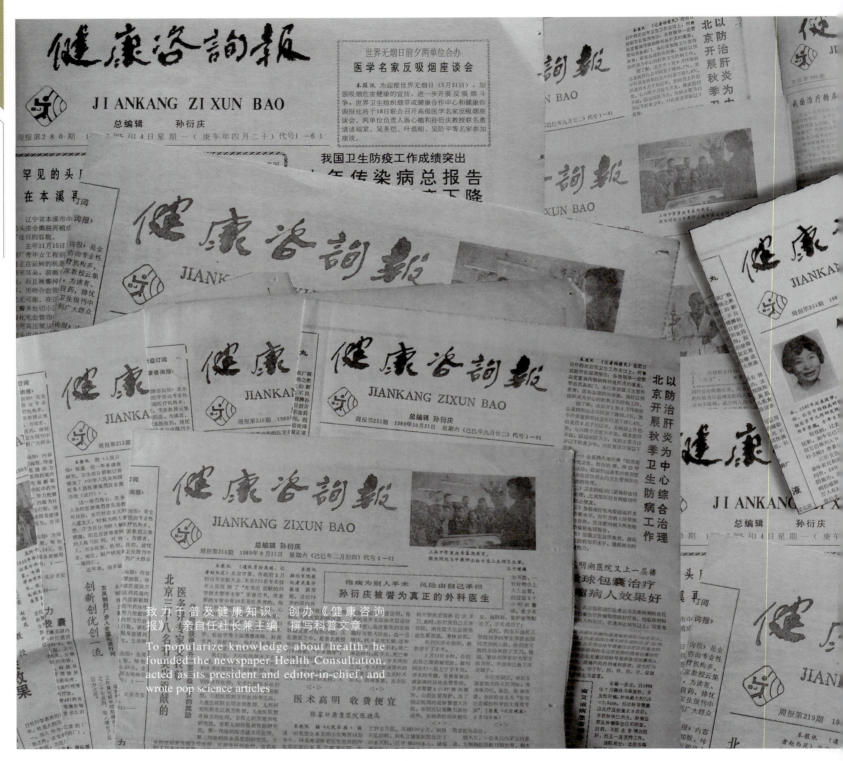

致力于普及健康知识，创办《健康咨询报》，亲自任社长兼主编，撰写科普文章

To popularize knowledge about health, he founded the newspaper Health Consultation, acted as its president and editor-in-chief, and wrote pop science articles

1991年11月11日在北京市科协第四次代表大会上与原北京市委书记李锡铭亲切握手

On November 11th, 1991, at the Fourth Congress of Beijing Science Association, he shook hands with Li Ximing, Party Secretary of Beijing

1986年与原卫生部长崔月犁合影

With former Health Minister Cui Yueli in 1986

1998年10月成立中美冠心病诊疗培训中心时与钱信忠老部长交谈

Conversing with former Minister Qian Xinzhong at the Sino-American Training Center for the Diagnosis and Treatment of Coronary Heart Diseases in October 1998

与原卫生部长崔月犁出席北京市中医和中西医结合工作会议

With former Public Health Minister Cui Yueli at the City of Beijing's Conference on Chinese Medicine and the Combination of Chinese and Western Medicine

1986年卫生工作会议

Health Care Conference, 1986

参加北京市医药顾问组座谈会

At the forum of the Beijing
Medical Consultation Group

参加北京市医院管理工作会议
At the Beijing's Conference on Hospital Administration

在卫生事业人才交流研讨会上讲话
Speech at the Seminar of Health Care Workers

140

连续六届被聘为北京市人民政府专家顾问团顾问

Engaged for six continuous sessions as a member of the Expert Advisory Body of the Municipal Government of Beijing

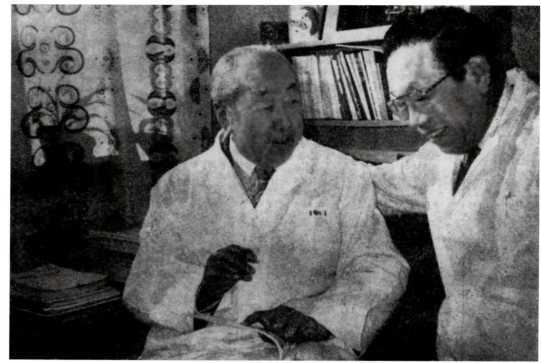

在老院长吴英恺家中亲切交谈

Conversing with former president Wu Yingkai in the latter's home

张兆光院长与前任院长吴英恺、孙衍庆向原副市长白介夫汇报安贞医院发展前景

President Zhang Zhaoguang and his predecessors, Wu Yingkai and Sun Yanqing, were reporting to former vice mayor Bai Jiefu about the prospect of Anzhen Hospital

与张兆光院长在一起
With President Zhang Zhaoguang

孙衍庆教授、张兆光院长与外宾亲切交谈

Professor Sun Yanqing and President Zhang Zhaoguang were talking with foreign visitors

励精图治　谋利于民 Vigorous efforts for the benefit of the people

安贞医院建院10周年时著名心胸外科专家苏鸿熙教授来院祝贺

Prof. Su Hongxi, Famous cardiothoracic surgery expert, came to Anzhen Hospital to congratulate on its 10th anniversary

1989年与澳门南光集团公司合作，引进先进设备，在安贞医院成立国际血液净化中心

In 1989, cooperating with Nam Kwong Group Company, Macau, Anzhen Hospital introduced advanced equipment and established its International Hemodialysis Center

与原北京市卫生局长金大鹏
在一起

With former Beijing Public
Health Bureau Chief Jin
Dapeng

与王宝恩教授在钟惠澜教授
百年诞辰会场

With Prof. Wang Bao'en at
the celebration of the 100th
birthday of Prof. Zhong Huilan

孙衍庆

励精图治 谋利于民 Vigorous efforts for the benefit of the people

2007年3月参加安贞医院新门诊综合楼奠基仪式

At the foundation-stone-laying ceremony for the new outpatient services building of Anzhen Hospital in March 2007

2008年记者联谊会与记者合影

With journalists at a press party in 2008

北京安贞医院建院25周年庆典与领导班子合影

With the leadership of Beijing Anzhen Hospital at
the celebration for its 25th anniversary

**148**

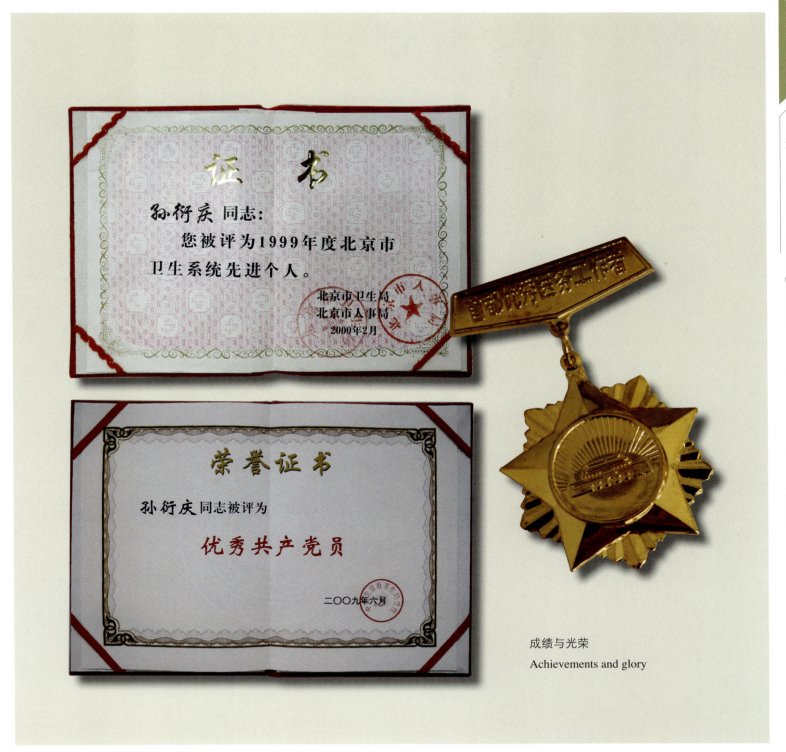

证　书

孙衍庆 同志：

您被评为1999年度北京市卫生系统先进个人。

北京市卫生局
北京市人事局
2000年2月

荣誉证书

孙衍庆 同志被评为

优秀共产党员

二〇〇九年六月

成绩与光荣

Achievements and glory

江上遥看隔秋云

多情不改年年色

千古芳心扮增君

岁月·人生

Personal
life

新诗已旧不堪闻

2004年3月在安贞医院老年保健中心成立大会
上与卫生部老部长钱信忠合影

With former Minister of Public Health Qian
Xinzhong at the inauguration of Anzhen
Hospital's Geriatric Healthcare Center in March
2004

2007年春节院领导班子来家中拜年

Courtesy call paid by the hospital leadership during the 2007 Spring Festival

卫生局赵春惠副局长来家中拜年

Courtesy call paid by deputy director of the Beijing Public Health Bureau

---

与夫人、同学严仁莲（1987年逝世）合影

With his wife(also his classmate) Yan Renlian, who passed way in 1987

乐在书中
The pleasure of reading

淡泊宁静
Tranquility

坚持在家中锻炼身体
Exercising at home

学者风范
Scholarly demeanor

在意大利

In Italy

158

在德国马克思和恩格斯坐像前

In front of the sitting statue of Marx and Engels in Germany

在法国巴黎凯旋门前

In front of the Arch of Triumph in Paris

参加卢森堡世界原子能学会

At the International Atomic Energy Society in Luxembourg

在美国纽约世贸大厦前

In front of the World Trade
Center in New York

在福建鼓浪屿岛

At Gulangyu Island, Fujian

在日本周总理纪念碑前

In front of the monument to Premier Zhou Enlai
in Japan

**161**

参观正在建设中的
"鸟巢"
Visiting the Bird's Nest
under construction

征服"好汉坡"
Conquering Hero
Slope

162

伉俪情深

A loving couple

全家福

The whole family

手足之情
Brotherhood

其乐融融
Enjoy a happy life

# 论文目录

## 一、普外、麻醉相关文章

| | | | | |
|---|---|---|---|---|
| 1. | 关于肺切除术的局部麻醉问题 | 孙衍庆 | 北京苏联红十字医院科学与实际工作论文集Ⅲ卷.人民卫生出版社 | 1958：103 |
| 2. | 局部麻醉在胸部外科之应用? | 孙衍庆 | 中华外科杂志 | 1954（1）：60—65 |
| 3. | 创伤和术后呼吸窘迫综合征的诊断和治疗 | 金旦年，孙衍庆 | 中华外科杂志 | 1980（2） |
| 4. | 外科的进展——癌的免疫疗法 | 孙衍庆，译<br>吴阶平，校 | 国际外科学杂志 | 1978（3）：3—4 |
| 5. | 高选择性迷走神经切断术 | 孙衍庆，译 | 国际外科学杂志 | 1977（1）：25 |
| 6. | 多发性内分泌性腺瘤病Ⅱa和Ⅱb型 | 孙衍庆，鲁泽清 | 国际外科学杂志 | 1976（5）：200—206 |
| 7. | 高度选择性迷走神经切断术不附加引流治疗十二指肠溃疡病的早期效果 | 孙衍庆，摘译<br>鲁泽清，校 | 国际外科学杂志 | 1974（2）：66 |
| 8. | 必须重阑尾切除术术后并发症对阑尾切除术某些技术问题的商讨 | 孙衍庆，孙福尧 | 中华外科杂志 | 1966,14（2）：73 |
| 9. | 有关临床复苏的某些问题 | 金旦年，孙衍庆 | 北京医学 | 1965,2：62—66 |
| 10. | 非融合型横过异位肾的手术复位治疗 | 孙衍庆，王澎，吴克让 | 中华外科杂志 | 1965,13（6）：515—517 |
| 11. | 正肾上腺素所致缺血皮肤坏死及其防治 | 孙衍庆，金旦年 | 中华医学杂志 | 1961,5：304—307 |
| 12. | 重症甲状腺机能亢进手术前后的处理 | 张双全，孙衍庆 | 中华外科杂志 | 1965,13（11）：969—971 |
| 13. | 恶性滑膜瘤一例介绍 | 孙衍庆 | 北京苏联红十字医院科学与实际工作论文集Ⅰ卷.人民卫生出版社 | 1956：153 |
| 14. | 介绍一种简易组织埋藏法 | 纳·依·纳格尼别达，杨天豪，孙衍庆 | 中华外科杂志 | 1956（1）：31—33 |
| 15. | 囊性卵巢畸胎瘤化脓而在右上腹部形成瘘管 | 孙衍庆 | 中华妇产科杂志 | 1955（1）：80—81 |
| 16. | 局部麻醉在胸部外科的应用（附二例报告） | 孙衍庆 | 中华外科杂志 | 1954（1）：603 |

| 17. | 局部麻醉在胸部外科中的应用 | 孙衍庆 | 中华外科杂志 | 1954（1）：47 |
|---|---|---|---|---|
| 18. | 高选择性迷走神经切断术治疗十二指肠溃疡62例临床报告 | 高东宸，王宇，孙衍庆 | 北京医学 | 1991，13(4)：210-212 |
| 19. | 原子吸收分光光度法测定健康犬血清和肝脏锌、铜含量 | 刘鸣，张健美，孙衍庆 | 首都医科大学学报 | 1988（1）：46-48 |
| 20. | 成人急性呼吸功能不全的诊断与治疗——近年文献综述 | 孙衍庆，朱大雷 | 国际外科学杂志 | 1980（1）：8-13 |

## 二、肝胆外科相关文章

| 1. | 肝上型门静脉高压症——布—加综合征 | 孙衍庆 | 门静脉高压症的外科治疗研究.北京出版社 | 1997：340-363 |
|---|---|---|---|---|
| 2. | EFFECTS OF SIDE-TO-SIDE PORTACAVAL SHUNT ON SERUM AND LIVER ZINC AND COPPER CONCENTTATIONS AND THEIR CORRECTION | Liu Ming, Zhang Jianmei, Sun Yanqing | Chinese Medical Journal | 1988，101(4):267-271 |
| 3. | HEMODYNAMICS OF LIMITED SIDE-TO-SIDE PORTACAVAL SHUNT (LPCS) AND THE SELECTION OF OPTIMAL STOMAL SIZE:AN EXPERIMENTAL STUDY | Sun Yanqing, Zhang Jianmei, Liu Chuanshou | Proceedings Of The International Symposium On Vascular Surgery | 1987:275 |
| 4. | AN EXPERIENCE OF USING UMITED SIDE-SIDE PORTACAVAL SHUNT IN TREATING PORTAL HYPERTENSION OVER 20 YEARS-AN ANALYSIS OF THE RESULTS OVER 310 CASES | Sun Yanching, Zhang Jianmei, Wang Yu | 中法外科学术讨论会 | 1982：26-27 |
| 5. | FACTORS INFLUENCING THE OCCURRENCE OF ENCEPHALOPATHY AFTER LIMITED SIDE-TO-SIDE PORTACAVAL SHUNT | Zhang Jianmei, Liu Ming, Sun Yanqing | Proceedings Of The International Symposium On Vascular Surgery | 1987:276 |
| | EFFECTS OF SIDE-TO-SIDE PORTACAVAL SHUNT ON SERUM AND LIVER ZINC AND COPPER CONCENTTATIONS AND ITS CORRECTION:EXPERIMENTS AND CLINICAL TRIALS | Liu Ming, Zhang Jianmei, Sun Yanqing | Proceedings Of The International Symposium On Vascular Surgery | 1987：277 |

| 6. | 限制性门腔静脉侧侧分流术的血液动力学与最佳吻合口径的选择 | 刘传绶，张健美，孙衍庆 | 中华外科杂志 | 1986，24(1)：44—48 |
|---|---|---|---|---|
| 7. | 门静脉高压症研究概况 | 孙衍庆 | 中国医学科学年鉴 | 1986：193—194 |
| 8. | 布——加氏综合征的外科治疗（摘要） | 孙衍庆，李伟生，朱大雷，等 | 全国首届胸心血管外科学术会议论文摘要汇编 | 1985：264—265 |
| 9. | LIMITED SIDE-TO-SIDE PORTACAVAL SHUNT OVER 20 YEAR'S CLINICAL EXPERIENCE | Sun Yanqing, Zhang Jianmei, Wang Yu | Chinese Medical Journal | 1984 (1)：13—18 |
| 10. | 门体分流与脑病（文献综述） | 刘传绶，孙衍庆 | 国际外科学杂志 | 1984 (2)：68—70 |
| 11. | 急性限制性门腔静脉侧侧分流术降低急诊手术死亡率的经验 | 孙衍庆，张健美，王宇 | 友谊医刊 | 1984 (4)：1—6 |
| 12. | 介绍一种三翼无伤血管吻合钳（为门—体静脉吻合术设计）介绍一种连续门静脉压力测量法 | 孙衍庆<br>孙衍庆 | 中华外科杂志<br>中华外科杂志 | 1965 (13)：634<br>1965 (13)：1094 |
| 13. | 介绍一种平面半圆形剪刀 | 孙衍庆 | 中华外科杂志 | 1981 (19)：675 |
| 14. | 限制性门腔侧侧分流术治疗门静脉高压症 | 孙衍庆 | 门静脉高压症的外科治疗研究.北京出版社 | 1997：155—169 |
| 15. | 门腔静脉分流术治疗门静脉高压症 | 孙衍庆 | 门静脉高压症的外科治疗研究.北京出版社 | 1997：140—154 |
| 16. | 肝上型门脉高压症的诊断和外科治疗 | 孙衍庆，朱大雷，王天佑，等 | 北京医学 | 1983，5(2)：69—72 |
| 17. | 门腔高压症食管胃底曲张静脉破裂大出血的急诊处理 | 孙衍庆，张健美，王宇 | 中华外科杂志 | 1983，21(1)：42—44 |
| 18. | 自体静脉补片移植肝外胆管成形术的实验研究及临床观察 | 王宇，许元弟，孙衍庆，等 | 中华外科杂志 | 1983，21(12)：733—734 |
| 19. | 经胸腹膜后腔肝裸区径路治疗布——加氏综合征 | 孙衍庆，朱大雷 | 中华外科杂志 | 1982 (2)：107—109 |
| 20. | 布—加氏综合征——外科治疗的新径路 | 孙衍庆，朱大雷 | 友谊医刊 | 1982 (1)：8—16 |
| 21. | 门脉高压症动力学及其临床意义（文献综述） | 张健美，孙衍庆 | 国际外科学杂志 | 1982 (3)：153—156 |
| 22. | 限制性门腔静脉侧侧分流术治疗门静脉高压症的评价——202例择期手术的疗效分析 | 孙衍庆，王宇，姚泽如 | 中华外科杂志 | 1981，19 (4)：195—201 |

| 23. | 门体静脉分流术——过去，现在和将来 | 孙衍庆，译 | 国际外科学杂志 | 1981（2）.20—22 |
|---|---|---|---|---|
| 24. | 限制性门腔静脉侧侧分流术——为什么提出这样一个问题 | 孙衍庆，金旦年，张健美 | 中华医学杂志 | 1966，52（4）：231—236 |
| 25. | 关于外科治疗门脉高压症大出血病人的一些意见 | 金旦年，孙衍庆，张健美 | 北京医学 | 1965（1）：25—27 |
| 26. | 肝切除 | 孙衍庆，译 | 国际外科学杂志 | 1975（5）：205 |

## 三、周围血管外科相关文章

| 1. | 动静脉瘘 | 孙衍庆 | 小儿先天性心脏病学 | 1998：1012—1022 |
|---|---|---|---|---|
| 2. | 下腔静脉系平滑肌瘤病（附2例报告） | 孙衍庆，王天佑，张长淮，等 | 中华胸心血管外科杂志 | 1991，7(4)：196—198 |
| 3. | 血管外科的进展 | 孙衍庆 | 中国医学科学年鉴 | 1986：189—190 |
| 4. | 正常青年人足背和胫后动脉搏动缺失的调查 | 孙衍庆，朱大雷，吴兆荣，等 | 北京医学 | 1984（3）：6—9 |
| 5. | An Investigation Of The Distal Arterial Pulsation Of The Extremities And Their Positional Test In Young Chinese People | Sun Yanqing, Zhang Dalei | Occlusive arterial diseases of the lower limbs in young patients | 15，15—33 |
| 6. | Absent Dorsalis Pedis And Posterior Tibial Pulsations In Normal Young Chinese | Sun Yanqing, Zhang Dalei | Chinese Medical Journal | 1983（9）:643—646 |
| 7. | 我国正常青年人体位性桡动脉搏动减弱和消失阳性率的调查——974只上肢检查结果的分析 | 孙衍庆，朱大雷，李伟生，等 | 中华医学杂志 | 1983，63(5)：281—284 |
| 8. | 周围血管严重损伤的诊断与治疗 | 孙衍庆，朱大雷，罗先正 | 北京医学 | 1980，2(1)：8—11 |
| 9. | 下腔与髂股静脉血栓形成症 血栓闭塞性脉管炎的硫酸镁疗法 | 孙衍庆，等 纳·依·纳格尼别达，孙衍庆，肖梁，等 | 中华外科杂志 中华外科杂志 | 1966，14(1)：11 1956（2）：102 |

## 四、胸外科相关文章

| 1. | 乳糜胸及其外科治疗（胸导管结扎与壁层胸膜剥脱术的合并应用） | 孙衍庆，金旦年 | 中华外科杂志 | 1963，11(2)：148—151 |
|---|---|---|---|---|

| | | | | |
|---|---|---|---|---|
| 2. | 创伤和术后呼吸窘迫综合征的诊断和治疗 | 金旦年，孙衍庆 | 中华外科杂志 | 1980，18(2)：100—103 |
| 3. | 膈肌瓣贲门成形术治疗食管贲门失驰缓症 | 孙衍庆，朱大雷 | 中华外科杂志 | 1965，13(8)：718—720 |
| 4. | 良性上腔静脉阻塞综合征（附四例报告） | 翁心植，孙衍庆 | 中华医学杂志 | 1963，49(5)：287—290 |
| 5. | 支气管扩张症的外科治疗 | 孙衍庆，纳·依·纳格尼别达 | 北京苏联红十字医院科学与实际工作论文集II卷，北京人民卫生出版社. | 1957：120 |
| 6. | 根据北京苏联红十字医院的材料看肺切除术问题—初步报道 | 孙衍庆，纳·依·纳格尼别达 | 北京苏联红十字医院科学与实际工作论文集II卷，北京人民卫生出版社. | 1957：117 |
| 7. | 纵隔气造影在食管癌诊断中的临床意义 | 孙衍庆，金丹年，李松年，等 | 中华外科杂志 | 1962，70(9)：581—583 |
| 8. | 胸壁大块缺损的修复问题 | 孙衍庆，王天佑，朱大雷，等 | 胸心血管外科杂志 | 1986，2(2)：84—86 |
| 9. | 胸壁肿瘤与胸壁大块缺损的修复 | 孙衍庆 | 现代胸心外科学.人民军医出版社 | 2000：486—494 |
| 10. | 气管、支气管外科进展 | 孙衍庆 | 中国医学科学年鉴 | 1986：190—191 |
| 11. | 食管外科的进展 贲门切除后胃食管返流的临床研究——附加与不附加幽门成形术的比较 | 孙衍庆，林元璋 韩宝仁，孙衍庆 | 中国医学科学年鉴 胸心血管外科杂志 | 1986：191—193 1985，1(3)：152—156 |
| 12. | 纵隔肿块的诊断方法及其评价——160例的临床分析 | 孙衍庆，吴兆荣，朱大雷，等 | 北京医学 | 1985（5)：19—21+67 |
| 13. | 关于胸壁肿瘤的诊断问题（54例临床分析） 原发性纵隔肿瘤与囊肿的诊断与鉴别诊断 | 孙衍庆，王天佑，朱大雷，等 孙衍庆，吴兆荣，朱大雷，等 | 胸心血管外科杂志 中华外科杂志 | 1985，1(1)：40—44 1984，22(10)：581—583 |
| 14. | 胸廓出口综合征 | 孙衍庆 | 现代胸心外科学.人民军医出版社 | 2000：476—485 |
| 15. | 胸廓出口综合征诊断与治疗的几个问题 | 孙衍庆，朱大雷，李伟生，等 | 中华外科杂志 | 1982，20(7) |
| 16. | 锁骨下动脉窃血综合征（文献综述） | 孙衍庆 | 国际外科学杂志 | 1983（2)65—69 |
| 17. | 锁骨下动脉窃血综合征 | 孙衍庆，朱大雷，王天佑，等 | 中华外科杂志 | 1983，21(10)：614—617 |
| 18. | 胸心外科血管外科现状与进展 | 孙衍庆 | 中华医学会第二十一次全国会员代表大会医学进展资料汇编 | 1994：140—147 |

| 19. | 胸心手术后乳糜胸 | 王天佑，孙衍庆，朱大雷，等 | 中华外科杂志 | 1990,28（4）：218—219 |
| --- | --- | --- | --- | --- |
| 20. | 食管外科的趋向（文献综述） | 孙衍庆 | 国际外科学杂志 | 1983（6）：332—335 |
| 21. | 慢性化脓性脓胸的外科治疗<br>——105例病人的分析与建议<br>肺和隆突癌的切除 | 孙衍庆，朱大雷，吴兆荣，等<br>孙衍庆 | 友谊医刊<br><br>国际外科学杂志 | 1979：1—6<br><br>1979（1）：56—57 |
| 22. | 创伤性膈疝 | 孙衍庆，鲁泽清，摘译 | 国际外科学杂志 | 1977（2）：99—106 |
| 23. | 支气管成形术在肺癌治疗中的应用 | 孙衍庆，编译 | 国际外科学杂志 | 1978（3）：167—168 |
| 24. | 肺癌的临床表现 | 孙衍庆，摘译<br>鲁泽清，校 | 国际外科学杂志 | 1974（3）：114—119 |
| 25. | 急性气管支气管创伤性损伤的处理 | 孙衍庆，摘编 | 国际外科学杂志 | 1974（1）：20—24 |

## 五、心脏外科相关文章

| 1. | 关于慢性粘连性心包炎的外科治疗问题 | 纳·依·纳格尼别达，孙衍庆 | 北京苏联红十字医院科学与实际工作论文集II卷．人民卫生出版社 | 1957：108 |
| --- | --- | --- | --- | --- |
| 2. | 低温低流量分量灌注在心内直视手术的应用 | 孙衍庆，朱大雷 | 中华外科杂志 | 1964（12）：223—226 |
| 3. | 闭式与直视二尖瓣分界分离术的比较（65例手术及远期随访分析） | 孙衍庆，金旦年，朱大雷，等 | 中华外科杂志 | 1979 17(6)：451—453 |
| 4. | 二尖瓣替换术与重建术的比较<br>——连续80例二尖瓣手术适应证与效果的分析 | 孙衍庆 | 国际外科学杂志 | 1978（5）：56—57 |
| 5. | 高分子聚合物适度低架心脏异种生物瓣膜的制备和初步应用 | 孙衍庆，朱大雷，董培青，等 | 北京医学 | 1981，3(3)：129—132 |
| 6. | 左心房折叠术在二尖瓣病变合并巨大左心房治疗中的应用 | 郑斯宏，孙衍庆，孟旭，等 | 中华外科杂志 | 2005,43(14)：918—920 |
| 7. | 延伸入右心房内肿瘤的外科治疗 | 伯平，张健群，孙衍庆，等 | 中国胸心血管外科临床杂志 | 2004,11(2)：141—142 |
| 8. | 巨大右冠状动脉瘤伴右冠左室瘘1例 | 孙衍庆，许尚栋，张宏家 | 中华胸心血管外科杂志 | 2003,19(3)：171 |
| 9. | 147例原发心脏肿瘤外科治疗的近远期效果 | 侯晓彤，孙衍庆，陈宝田，等 | 中华胸心血管外科杂志 | 2002,18（3）：155—157 |
| 10. | 机械心脏人工瓣膜 | 郑斯宏，孙衍庆 | 世界医疗器械 | 2002（8）：13—17 |

| | | | | |
|---|---|---|---|---|
| 11. | 生物组织心脏人工瓣膜 | 孙衍庆 | 世界医疗器械 | 2002（8）：20—22 |
| 12. | 组织工程人工心脏瓣膜的研究进程 | 张宏家，孙衍庆 | 世界医疗器械 | 2002（8）：24—26 |
| 13. | 激光心肌血运重建的临床研究 | 屈正，<br>张兆光，孙衍庆，等 | 中国激光医学杂志 | 2001,10(3)：192 |
| 14. | 慢性心房纤颤及其外科治疗 | 李潮，孙衍庆 | 人民军医出版社 | 2000：1316—1318 |
| 15. | 左心发育不良综合症 | 李潮，孙衍庆 | 现代胸心外科学 | 2000：1183—1189 |
| 16. | 巨左心房症 | 孙衍庆 | 现代胸心外科学 | 2000：1389—1397 |
| 17. | 慢性特发性心包积液症 | 李潮，孙衍庆 | 现代胸心外科学.<br>人民军医出版社 | 2000：1567—1570 |
| 18. | 先天性主动脉瓣上狭窄的外科治疗 | 董然，<br>陈宝田，孙衍庆，等 | 中国胸心血管外科临床杂志 | 2000,7(2)：126—127 |
| 19. | 激光心肌血运重建的现状及临床应用的结果与体会 | 屈正，<br>孙衍庆，张兆光，等 | 激光心肌打孔血运重建术专题报告会 | 1998 |
| 20. | 冠心病外科治疗的最新进展——兼论激光打孔心肌血运重建术 | 孙衍庆 | 北京市冠心病治疗进展会上的报告 | 1995.10 |
| 21. | 146例风湿性二尖瓣病变伴重度肺动脉高压外科治疗效果分析 | 屈正，<br>孙衍庆，李平，等 | 庆祝安贞医院成立十三周年万例体外循环心血管手术及有关问题交流论文集 | 1997：69 |
| 22. | 窦性心律重建手术 | 孙衍庆，<br>李潮，林元璋 | 中华胸心血管外科杂志 | 1996,12(5)：284—286 |
| 23. | 激光心肌打孔血运重建术的研究与应用现状 | 屈正，<br>张兆光，孙衍庆 | 中华胸心血管外科杂志 | 1990,12(5)：259—261 |
| 24. | 慢性心房纤颤的外科治疗 | 李潮，孙衍庆 | 中华胸心血管外科杂志 | 1996,12(5)：259—261 |
| 25. | 小循环心功能无创检测法评价二尖瓣手术效果的初步观察 | 屈正，<br>孙衍庆，陈英淳，等 | 首届国际小循环无创检测（右胸电导纳容积波法）心功能学术研讨会 | 1996：78—82 |
| 26. | Psychiatric Disturbance After Open-Heart Surgery | Sun Yanqing,<br>Wang Tianyou,<br>Cheng Shuen | International Conference On Intensive And Critical Care For Thoracic And Cardiovascular Surgical Patients | 87 |
| 27. | 巨左房及其外科治疗 | 孙衍庆，<br>王天佑，朱大雷，等 | 心肺血管病杂志 | 1986（2）：24 |

| | | | | |
|---|---|---|---|---|
| 28. | 带瓣人工血管替换升主动脉主动脉瓣和冠状动脉移植术 | 孙衍庆，王天佑，陈宝田 | 心肺血管病杂志 | 1986 (2)：23 |
| 29. | 瓣膜手术前后小循环心功能无创检测法各项参数的改变及其临床意义 | 屈正，孙衍庆，陈英淳 | 首届国际小循环无创检测（右胸电导纳容积波法）心功能学术研讨会1996 | 1996：91－95 |
| 30. | 精简迷宫手术治疗慢性心房纤颤 | 孙衍庆，李潮，林元璋 | 全国生物心脏瓣膜学术研讨会 | 1995：56－58 |
| 31. | 同种异体大血管移植治疗小儿复杂先天性心脏病 | 孙衍庆，杨能善，罗毅，等 | 心肺血管病杂志 | 1994，13(1)：6－9 |
| 32. | 冠状动脉旁路移植术16例临床分析 | 王天佑，孙衍庆，李卫生，等 | 中国循环杂志 | 1994，9(9)：532－534 |
| 33. | THE EXPERIMENTAL STUDY OF RETROGRADE CEREBRAL PERFUSION THROUGH THE SUPERIOR VENA CAVA FOR PROTECTING THE BRAIN DURING DEEO HYPOTHERMIA AND CIRCULATORY ARREST | Yang Chuanrui, Sun Yanching, Dong Peiqing, et al. | Practice And Research Thoracic And Cardiovascular Surgery And Extracorporeal Circulation Proceedings Of The International Conference | 1994：448 |
| 34. | THE CHANGES OF LIPID PEROXIDATION AND PATHOLOGY IN COLLAPSED LUNG BEFORE AND AFTER LEFT HEART BYPASS-EXPERIMENTAL STUDY | Qu Zheng, Sun Yanqing, Dong Peiqing, et al. | Practice And Research Thoracic And Cardiovascular Surgery And Extracorporeal Circulation Proceedings Of The International Conference | 1994：513 |
| 35. | 钛镍记忆合金环在主动脉移植外科应用的实验研究（结扎法） | 杨传瑞，孙衍庆，董培青，等 | 中华胸心血管外科杂志 | 1993，9(2)：158－160 |
| 36. | 深低温停循环下的脑损伤和保护 | 林元璋，孙衍庆，杨能善 | 中华胸心血管外科杂志 | 1993，9(1)：86－88 |
| 37. | 深低温停循环及脑灌注有关脑保护问题（文献综述） | 杨传瑞，孙衍庆，董培青 | 国际外科学杂志 | 1993 (3)：155－158 |
| 38. | 112例主动脉瓣二尖瓣双瓣膜替换术临床分析 | 陈宝田，孙衍庆，李平，等 | 中华胸心血管外科杂志 | 1992，8(1)：14－16 |
| 39. | 矫正型大动脉转位左侧房室瓣替换术2例 | 孙衍庆，宫殿富 | 中华胸心血管外科杂志 | 1992，8(3)：196－197 |
| 40. | 巨大心脏病人的瓣膜置换 | 陈宝田，孙衍庆，李平，等 | 中华外科杂志 | 1991，29(3)：188－189 |
| 41. | 心肌保护及体外循环专题学术会议内容概要 | 苏鸿熙，孙衍庆，薛淦兴 | 中华胸心血管外科杂志 | 1990，6(1)：2－4 |

| 42. | 103例心瓣膜病主动脉瓣及二尖瓣双瓣置换术的临床研究 | 陈宝田，孙衍庆，李平，等 | 心肺血管学报 | 1989,8(2)：75—79 |
| --- | --- | --- | --- | --- |
| 43. | 106例婴儿和幼儿先天性心脏病的外科治疗 | 孙衍庆，杨能善，邵燕夫，等 | 全国第二届胸心血管外科学术会议论文摘要汇编 | 1989：97 |
| 44. | 体外循环心脏直视手术后精神障碍 | 孙衍庆，王天佑，陈淑恩 | 胸心血管外科杂志 | 1987,3(4)：213—215 |
| 45. | 自体肺氧合在直视心脏手术中的应用 | 董培青，孙衍庆 | 国外医学外科学分册 | 1987,5：275—277 |
| 46. | 心脏直视手术后的心律失常与处理 | 陈淑恩，孙衍庆 | 北京医学 | 1987,9(3)：155—158 |
| 47. | 心肌保护的研究近况：药物对心肌的保护作用（文献综述） | 韩宝仁，孙衍庆 | 国际外科学杂志 | 1985（1）：3—6 |
| 48. | 心肌保护的研究近况：有关心停搏液的问题 | 韩宝仁，孙衍庆 | 国际外科学杂志 | 1984（3）：155—158 |
| 49. | 高分子聚合物适度低架心脏异种生物瓣膜的制备和初步应用 | 孙衍庆，朱大雷，董培青，等 | 北京医学 | 1981（3）：3—6 |
| 50. | 动脉导管未闭手术后的高血压症及其临床意义 | 孙衍庆，金旦年 | 中华外科杂志 | 1966（14）：382 |
| 51. | 万例体外循环心血管手术临床分析研究 | 张兆光，孙衍庆，李平，等 | 庆祝安贞医院成立十三周年万例体外循环心血管手术及有关问题交流论文集 | 1997：1—11 |
| 52. | 冠心病治疗进展及TMLR在冠心病治疗中的地位 | 孙衍庆 | 激光心肌打孔血运重建术专题报告会 | 1998 |
| 53. | 激光心肌血运重建术治疗冠心病的临床体会 | 屈正，张兆光，孙衍庆，等 | 中华胸心血管外科杂志 | 1999,15(5)：266—268 |
| 54. | 激光心肌血运重建术治疗冠心病的临床观察 | 屈正，张兆光，孙衍庆，等 | 中华医学杂志 | 2000,80(1)：43—44 |
| 55. | 77例激光心肌血运重建术疗效研究 | 屈正，张兆光，孙衍庆，等 | 中国激光医学杂志 | 2000,9(3)：191 |
|  | 激光心肌血运重建术疗效分析 | 屈正，张兆光，孙衍庆，等 | 中华外科杂志 | 2000,38(9)：665—668 |
| 56. | 主动脉缩窄的诊断和外科治疗 | 郑斯宏，孙衍庆，陈宝田，等 | 中华医学杂志 | 1999,79(10)：747—748 |
| 57. | 经皮主动脉覆膜支架植入治疗巨大动脉导管1例 | 李海洋，张宏家，孙衍庆，等 | 中华胸心血管外科杂志 | 2006,22(5)：325 |
| 58. | KATP通道开放剂与心肌保护 | 侯晓彤，孙衍庆 | 中华胸心血管外科杂志 | 2000,16(1)：62—63 |

| | | | |
|---|---|---|---|
| 59. | 我国心血管外科学学科的形成与现状 | 孙衍庆 | 中华外科杂志 | 1991,29(11)：662-665 |
| 60. | 全心外右心旁路手术 | 王维新，孙衍庆 | 中华胸心血管外科杂志 | 1999,15(6)：376-378 |
| 61. | 细胞内液型胶体液HBS对离体心脏的长期保存作用 | 郑斯宏，孙衍庆，林阳，等 | 中华胸心血管外科杂志 | 1999,15(1)：51-54 |
| 62. | 主动脉缩窄术后高血压的发生率和治疗 | 郑斯宏，孙衍庆，陈宝田，等 | 第四军医大学学报 | 1999（8）：封2 |
| 63. | 心脏大血管外科的现状与发展趋势 | 孙衍庆 | 庆祝安贞医院成立十三周年万例体外循环心血管手术及有关问题交流论文集 | 1997：11 |
| 64. | 146例严重肺动脉高压者二尖瓣替换术疗效分析 | 屈正，孙衍庆，陈英淳，等 | 中华胸心血管外科杂志 | 1998,14(6)：330-333 |
| 65. | 孪生兄弟同患主动脉瓣及瓣上狭窄的治疗与病因 | 谢进生，孙衍庆，杨焕明，等 | 中华胸心血管外科杂志 | 1998,14(3)：133-135 |
| 66. | 瓣叶延伸复位术治疗三尖瓣下移畸形 | 李潮，孙衍庆，毕六一，等 | 中华胸心血管外科杂志 | 1998,14(4)：231 |
| 67. | 单肺通气左心转流萎陷侧肺损伤的实验研究 | 屈正，孙衍庆，董培青，等 | 心肺血管病杂志 | 1997,16(3)：231-233 |
| 68. | 二尖瓣替换术后房颤转复为窦性心律的临床分析 | 侯晓彤，孙衍庆，李潮，等 | 心肺血管病杂志 | 1997,16(2)：124-126 |
| 69. | 单肺通气并左心转流前后两侧肺组织生化及形态学改变的实验观察 | 屈正，孙衍庆，董培青，等 | 中国循环杂志 | 1998,13(2)：114-116 |
| 70. | 心脏大血管外科的现状与发展趋势 | 孙衍庆 | 心肺血管病杂志 | 1997,16(4)：248-253 |
| 71. | 万例体外循环心血管手术临床资料分析报告 | 张兆光，孙衍庆，李平，等 | 心肺血管病杂志 | 1997,16(4)：243-247 |
| 72. | 右胸电导纳容积图（小循环心功能测试）法评价二尖瓣手术效果初步报告 | 屈正，孙衍庆，陈英淳，等 | 中华胸心血管外科杂志 | 1997,13(4)：217-219 |
| 73. | 心脏直视手术外源性磷酸肌酸的心肌保护效果 | 董培青，孙衍庆，李潮，等 | 中华胸心血管外科杂志 | 1997,13(4)：212-214 |
| 74. | 深低温停循环期间经上腔静脉逆行灌注脑保护的动物实验及临床摘要 | 杨传瑞，孙衍庆，董培青 | 庆祝安贞医院成立十三周年万例体外循环心血管手术及有关问题交流论文集 | 1997：105 |
| 75. | 钛镍记忆合金环在主动脉移植外科应用的实验研究（结扎法） | 杨传瑞，孙衍庆，董培青 | 庆祝安贞医院成立十三周年万例体外循环心血管手术及有关问题交流论文集 | 1997：106 |

| 76. | 心脏直视手术外源性磷酸肌酸的心肌保护效果 | 董培青，孙衍庆，李潮，等 | 中华胸心血管外科杂志 | 1997,13(4)：212—214 |
|---|---|---|---|---|
| 77. | 深低温停循环期间经上腔静脉逆行灌注脑保护的动物实验及临床摘要 | 杨传瑞，孙衍庆，董培青 | 庆祝安贞医院成立十三周年万例体外循环心血管手术及有关问题交流论文集 | 1997：105 |
| 78. | 钛镍记忆合金环在主动脉移植外科应用的实验研究（结扎法） | 杨传瑞，孙衍庆，董培青 | 庆祝安贞医院成立十三周年万例体外循环心血管手术及有关问题交流论文集 | 1997：106 |
| 79. | 左心转流萎陷肺损伤及其保护的实验与临床研究（摘要） | 屈正，孙衍庆，董培青，等 | 庆祝安贞医院成立十三周年万例体外循环心血管手术及有关问题交流论文集 | 1997：106 |
| 80. | 二尖瓣替换术后房颤自动转复为窦性心律的临床分析 | 侯晓彤，孙衍庆，李潮，等 | 庆祝安贞医院成立十三周年万例体外循环心血管手术及有关问题交流论文集 | 1997：73 |
| 81. | 先天性主动脉瓣上狭窄的诊断及外科治疗 | 董然，陈宝田，孙衍庆，等 | 庆祝安贞医院成立十三周年万例体外循环心血管手术及有关问题交流论文集 | 1997：46 |

## 六、主动脉外科（含夹层动脉瘤）相关文章

| 1. | 我国心脏——主动脉和主动脉疾病外科的发展 | 孙衍庆 | 医学研究通讯 | 2005,34(3)：6—10 |
|---|---|---|---|---|
| 2. | 应用左心转流术的降主动脉瘤手术治疗 | 董培青，孙衍庆，屈正，等 | 中华胸心血管外科杂志 | 1995,11(3)：129—130 |
| 3. | 白塞氏病合并升主动脉瘤和主动脉关闭不全的外科治疗——个案报告与文献复习 | 刘愚勇，孙衍庆，蔡克强 | 心肺血管病杂志 | 2002,21(4)：214—216 |
| 4. | BAII型国产覆膜支架在犬腹主动脉瘤模型中的应用 | 许尚栋，孙衍庆，王贵生，等 | 中华实验外科杂志 | 2002,19(5)：409—412 |
| 5. | 胸主动脉瘤和主动脉夹层动脉瘤外科治疗不同术式的评价 | 孙衍庆 | 第二届五洲国际心血管病研讨会学术论文汇编 | 2002：20—21 |
| 6. | 大动脉覆膜支架介入治疗降主动脉假性及夹层动脉瘤 | 许尚栋，孙衍庆，杜家会 | 第二届五洲国际心血管病研讨会学术论文汇编 | 2002：28—31 |
| 7. | 主动脉根部瘤和升主动脉瘤的外科治疗 | 孙衍庆，张宏家 | 第十三届全国心脏外科专题研讨会论文汇编 | 2002：5—7 |
| 8. | 主动脉瘤的血管内支架治疗 | 李潮，孙衍庆 | 心肺血管病杂志 | 2001,20(1)：62—63 |

| 9. | 主动脉根部病变的外科治疗 | 段明科，孙衍庆 | 中国综合临床 | 2000,16(9)：646-647 |
|---|---|---|---|---|
| 10. | The Thoracic Aortic Aneurysm And Dissection:Surgical Results And Experience Of 428 Cases | Sun Yanqing | The Fifth China International Congress On Thoracic And Cardiovascular Surgery | 2000:42-43 |
| 11. | 胸部降主动脉瘤的外科治疗 | 王京生，孙衍庆，刘传绶,等 | 中华胸心血管外科杂志 | 1999,15(2)：114 |
| 12. | 共同动脉干畸形 | 孙衍庆 | 小儿先天性心脏病学 | 1998：880-895 |
| 13. | 先天性主动脉缩窄 | 孙衍庆 | 小儿先天性心脏病学 | 1998：944-958 |
| 14. | 左心转流降主动脉瘤手术中致萎陷肺损伤因素的临床研究 | 屈正，孙衍庆，董培青,等 | 中华胸心血管外科杂志 | 1997,13(3)：151-153 |
| 15. | 胸部主动脉瘤的外科治疗 | 王京生，孙衍庆，刘传绶,等 | 中华外科杂志 | 1997,35(5)：289-291 |
| 16. | 深低温停循环上腔静脉逆行灌注在主动脉瘤手术中的应用 | 孙衍庆，董培青，杨传瑞,等 | 中华胸心血管外科杂志 | 1994,10(1)：25-29 |
| 17. | Extracorporeal Circulation for Great Vessels Surgery:A Review of 131 Cases | Dong Peiqing, Sun Yanqing, Yang Jing,et al. | The Journal Of Extra-Corporeal Technology | 1995,27:216-220 |
| 18. | 左心房压增高对血管紧张素转换酶影响的实验观察 | 屈正，孙衍庆，谭一忠,等 | 心肺血管病杂志 | 1995,14(2)：97-98 |
| 19. | Experimental study of a new sutureless intraluminal graft with a shape-memory alloy ring | Yang Chuanrui, Sun Yanqing, Dong Peiqing,et al. | J THORAC CARDIOVASC SURG | 1994,107:191-5 |
| 20. | SURGICAL TREATMENT OF THORACIC AORTIC ANEURYSM | Wang JingSheng, Sun YanQing, Liu ChuanShou,et al. | Practice And Research Thoracic And Cardiovascular Surgery And Extracorporeal Cirvulation Proceedings Of The International Conference | 1994:243-247 |
| 21. | 离心泵在胸主动脉瘤手术中的应用 | 屈正，孙衍庆，董培青 | 国际外科学杂志 | 1993 (3)：277-278 |
| 22. | 胸主动脉瘤217例手术回顾与分析（摘要） | 孙衍庆，李潮，周其文 | 庆祝安贞医院成立十三周年万例体外循环心血管手术及有关问题交流论文集 | 1997:88 |
| 23. | 胸主动脉瘤手术中肺损伤因素的探讨及前瞻性研究（摘要） | 屈正，孙衍庆，董培青,等 | 庆祝安贞医院成立十三周年万例体外循环心血管手术及有关问题交流论文集 | 1997:87 |
| | 胸降主动脉瘤的外科治疗 | 李潮，孙衍庆，林元璋,等 | 庆祝安贞医院成立十三周年万例体外循环心血管手术及有关问题交流论文集 | 1997:88 |

| 24. | 胸腹主动脉瘤手术脊髓损伤研究现状 | 屈正，孙衍庆 | 中华胸心血管外科杂志 | 1995（3）：184—185 |
| --- | --- | --- | --- | --- |
| 25. | 家兔拟主动脉瘤手术单肺通气模型 | 屈正，孙衍庆，谭一忠，等 | 心肺血管病杂志 | 1995,14(1):44—45 |
| 26. | 对MRA诊断主动脉夹层动脉瘤的评价（附136例报告） | 张宏家，孙衍庆，范占祥，等 | 中华胸心血管外科杂志 | 2006,22(3)：155—157 |
| 27. | 覆膜支架介入治疗降主动脉假性及夹层动脉瘤八例 | 许尚栋，孙衍庆，杜嘉会，等 | 中华医学杂志 | 2003,83(10)：883—884 |
| 28. | 腔内覆膜支架隔绝术在夹层动脉瘤治疗中的应用 | 张宏家，孙衍庆，刘愚勇，等 | 第四届五洲国际心血管病研讨会论文汇编 | 2006:232 |
| 29. | Stanford A型主动脉夹层的外科治疗 | 郑斯宏，孙衍庆，孟旭，等 | 中华外科杂志 | 2005,43(18)：1177—1180 |
| 30. | 主动脉夹层动脉瘤形成的生物力学机制的实验研究——主动脉在体运动与动态变形分析 | 张宏家，孙衍庆，李晓阳，等 | 北京生物医学工程 | 2005,124(13)：166—170 |
| 31. | Stanford A型主动脉夹层手术中股动脉插管的应用 | 侯晓彤，孙衍庆，张宏家，等 | 心肺血管病杂志 | 2005,24(2):68—70 |
| 32. | 甲基强的松龙和吲哚美辛对大鼠腹主动脉瘤的防治作用 | 李卫民，孙衍庆 | 天津医药 | 2005,33(3)：164—167 |
| 33. | 胸主动脉瘤和主动脉夹层动脉瘤外科治疗不同术式的评价 | 孙衍庆 | 中国胸心血管外科临床杂志 | 2003,10(1)：1—2 |
| 34. | 支架型人工血管介入治疗主动脉夹层动脉瘤及主动脉穿透溃疡30例报告 | 许尚栋，孙衍庆，李志忠，等 | 心肺血管病杂志 | 2005,24(1)：5—7 |
| 35. | 胸主动脉夹层动脉瘤的外科治疗——手术适应证手术方法的选择及疗效 | 孙衍庆，张宏家，董培青，等 | 心肺血管病杂志 | 2003,22(1)：5—7 |
| 36. | 覆膜支架介入治疗慢性DeBakey Ⅲb型夹层动脉瘤的早期体会 | 许尚栋，孙衍庆，杜嘉会，等 | 中国医学影像技术 | 2002,18(2)：104—106 |
| 37. | 胸主动脉夹层动脉瘤的不典型核磁共振成像表现及其临床处理 | 谢进生，孙衍庆，刘愚勇，等 | 中华胸心血管外科杂志 | 2000,16(3)：174—175 |
| 38. | 经人工血管行股动脉插管在主动脉夹层手术中的应用 | 侯晓彤，孙衍庆，崔恒等 | 中华医学杂志 | 2002,82(5)：294—296 |
| 39. | 胸部主动脉内膜剥离症（胸主动脉夹层动脉瘤） | 孙衍庆 | 现代胸心外科学．人民军医出版社 | 2000：1462—1479 |
| 40. | DeBakey Ⅲ型夹层动脉瘤的治疗 | 王京生，孙衍庆，刘传绶，等 | 中国循环杂志 | 1998,13(3)：161—163 |
| 41. | 主动脉夹层动脉瘤 | 李茂亭，孙衍庆 | 心肺血管病杂志 | 1993,12(4)：255—257 |

| 42. | 胸主动脉夹层动脉瘤（57例手术治疗病人的分析） | 孙衍庆，王京生，李平，等 | 中华胸心血管外科杂志 | 1993,9(1)：1-5 |
| --- | --- | --- | --- | --- |
| 43. | 主动脉夹层动脉瘤的外科治疗 | 孙衍庆，朱大雷，王天佑，等 | 中华外科杂志 | 1984,22(11)：677-680 |

## 七、马凡综合征相关文章

| 1. | Marfan综合征所致升主动脉瘤与主动脉瓣关闭不全的手术治疗（二例报告） | 孙衍庆，王天佑 | 中华心血管杂志 | 1986,14(2)：80-82 |
| --- | --- | --- | --- | --- |
| 2. | 升主动脉瘤伴主动脉瓣关闭不全——25例手术结果 | 孙衍庆，陈宝田，李平，王天佑 | 中华胸心血管外科杂志 | 1989,5(2)：66-69 |
| 3. | 马方综合征 | 孙衍庆 | 现代胸心外科学 | 2000：1144-1158 |
| 4. | β受体阻滞剂治疗马方综合征主动脉根部扩张的临床观察 | 谢进生，裴金凤，孙衍庆，等 | 中国心血管病研究杂志 | 2006,4(5)：326-328 |
| 5. | 马方综合征主动脉根部瘤手术治疗84例经验 | 郑斯宏，孙衍庆，孟旭，等 | 中华医学杂志 | 2005,85(32)：2279-2282 |
| 6. | 带瓣人工血管替换升主动脉--主动脉瓣和冠状动脉移植术 | 孙衍庆，王天佑，陈宝田 | 胸心血管外科杂志 | 1996,2(1)：15-18 |
| 7. | 用新标准对76例马方综合征的诊断再分析 | 谢进生，孙衍庆，周子凡，等 | 中国循环杂志 | 2004,19(1)：59-61 |
| 8. | 儿童Marfan综合征的诊断和外科治疗 | 谢进生，史亚民，孙衍庆，等 | 中华小儿外科杂志 | 2004,25(1)：28-31 |
| 9. | 连续5例Cabrol手术治疗马凡综合征主动脉根部病变 | 张健群，孙衍庆，陈英淳，等 | 中华胸心血管外科杂志 | 1998,14(2)：75-78 |
| 10. | 马方综合征的外科治疗 | 王京生，孙衍庆，刘传绶，等 | 北京医科大学学报 | 1998,30(4)：353-354 |
| 11. | 儿童马凡综合征 | 孙衍庆，张健群 | 小儿先天性心脏病学 | 1998：1066-1080 |
| 12. | 1号原纤蛋白基因表达在马凡综合征的诊断和心血管病变确定中的应用性研究（摘要） | 谢进生，孙衍庆，李潮 | 庆祝安贞医院成立十三周年万例体外循环心血管手术及有关问题交流论文集 | 1997：89 |
| 13. | 马凡综合征与修订新标准——76例临床诊断分析（摘要） | 谢进生，孙衍庆，李潮，等 | 庆祝安贞医院成立十三周年万例体外循环心血管手术及有关问题交流论文集 | 1997：90 |
| | 马凡综合征妊娠的处理（摘要） | 谢进生，孙衍庆，毕六一 | 庆祝安贞医院成立十三周年万例体外循环心血管手术及有关问题交流论文集 | 1997：90 |
| 14. | Marfan综合征分子遗传学研究进展 | 谢进生，孙衍庆，黄尚志 | 中华医学遗传学杂志 | 1997,14(6)：276-279 |

| 15. | THE SURGERY AND SOME RELATED PROBLEMS OE MARFAN'S ANEURYSM | Sun Yanqing, Xie Jinsheng, Li Chao,et al. | Fourth International Congress On TCVS In China | 1997:A5—7 |
|---|---|---|---|---|
| 16. | BENTALL COMPOSITE GRAFT PROCEDURE ON MARFAN ANEURYSM OF ASCENDING AORTA--EXPERIENCE OF 105 CASES | Sun Yanqing, Liu Chuanshou, Zhou Qiwen,et al. | Practice And Research Thoracic And Cardiovascular Surgery And Extracorporeal Cirvulation Proceedings Of The International Conference | 1994:248 |
| 17. | 升主动脉根动脉瘤伴主动脉瓣关闭不全Bentall复合人工血管替换术——105例经验 | 孙衍庆,等 | 全国第10次心脏外科专题研讨会论文摘要汇编 | 1994:11 |
| 18. | 马凡综合征心脏大血管病变外科治疗中的问题与对策 | 孙衍庆,王天佑 | 中华外科杂志 | 1993,31(5):293—295 |
| 19. | Bentall 手术治疗马凡综合征心血管病变53例的个人经验分析 | 孙衍庆 | 心肺血管报 | 1991,10(3):168—172 |
| 20. | SURGICAL TREATMENT OF THE CARDIOVASCULAR DISEASE IN MARFAN'S SYNDROME--SIMPLE AORTIC REPLACEMENT VS BENTALL OPERATION | Sun Yanqing, Ping Li, Wang Tianyou, et al. | International Conference On Thoracin And Cardiovascular Surgery | 1986:191 |

## 八、辅助循环相关文章

| 1. | 自制微型轴流血泵对缺血后心脏左心辅助机制的实验研究 | 侯晓彤,蔺嫦燕,孙衍庆,等 | 中华实验外科杂志 | 2001,18(5):394—396 |
|---|---|---|---|---|
| 2. | 循环生物力学的模型研究 | 江朝光,姜澜,孙衍庆,等 | 军医进修学院学报 | 1999,20(4):241—244 |
| 3. | 流动显示技术在植入式微型血泵设计方案改进中的应用 | 李卫民,孙衍庆,蔺嫦燕 | 北京生物医学工程 | 1999,18(3):188—193 |
| 4. | 心室辅助装置的临床应用 | 侯晓彤,孙衍庆 | 中华胸心血管外科杂志 | 1999,15(4):253—255 |
| 5. | I型血泵左心辅助循环动物实验研究 | 蔺嫦燕,孙衍庆,侯晓彤,等 | 中国生物医学工程学报 | 1998,17(2):177—182 |
| 6. | 微型血泵的研制及其模拟实验研究 | 蔺嫦燕,孙衍庆,董培青,等 | 中国生物医学工程学报 | 1997,16(1):64—69 |
| 7. | 小型鼓泡型人工肺的研制 | 凤琪,孙衍庆 | 北京生物医学工程 | 1988,(Z1):60—64 |
| 8. | 不同体外循环方式在主动脉瘤外科手术中的应用 | 刘传绶,王京生,孙衍庆,等 | 中国循环杂志 | 1997,12(1):51—53 |

## 九、卫生事业管理、评议、回忆、纪念相关文章

| | | | | |
|---|---|---|---|---|
| 1. | 关于首都的卫生事业建设问题 | 孙衍庆 | | |
| 2. | 改革公费医疗与劳保医疗制度的设想 | 孙衍庆 | 中国医院管理 | 1991,11(1):11—16 |
| 3. | 创刊20周年贺词 | 苏鸿熙,孙衍庆 | 中华胸心血管外科杂志 | 2005,21(1):1 |
| 4. | 一位知名医学家的成功之路——在吴英恺教授八旬荣寿报告会上的讲话 | 孙衍庆 | | 1990:5 |
| 5. | 学习思考再读吴英恺院士的《谈医道》——悼念吴英恺院士 | 孙衍庆 | 中华胸心血管外科杂志 | 2004,20(1):2 |
| 6. | 在改革开放中快速成长——祝贺北京安贞医院建院二十周年 | 孙衍庆 | "我们一同走过"——安贞医院二十年专集 | 2004 |
| 7. | 学医从医五十年 | 孙衍庆 | 中国医院 | 2002,6(2):30—32 |
| 8. | 喜庆我国心脏移植新进展的思维 | 苏鸿熙,孙衍庆 | 中华胸心血管外科杂志 | 1994,10(1):1 |
| 9. | 十年回顾——纪念北京市心肺血管医疗研究中心建立十周年 | 吴英恺,孙衍庆,吴兆苏,等 | 心肺血管报 | 1991,10(3):129—133 |
| 10. | 中华医学会胸心血管外科学会成立大会及全国首届胸心血管外科学术会议总结 | 孙衍庆 | 胸心血管外科杂志 | 1986,2(1):3—5 |
| 11. | 科学的创新,世界的盛会先天性主动脉瓣下狭窄的外科治疗 | 孙衍庆 董然,陈宝田,孙衍庆,等 | 引进国外医药技术与设备庆祝安贞医院成立十三周年万例体外循环心血管手术及有关问题交流论文集 | 1999,5(7):10—11 1997:49 |
| | 慢性心房纤颤的外科治疗——窦性心律重建手术 | 李潮,孙衍庆 | 庆祝安贞医院成立十三周年万例体外循环心血管手术及有关问题交流论文集 | 1997:67 |

## 编后语

　　2009年，对于孙衍庆老院长而言，有着十分特殊的意义。其一，适逢中华人民共和国成立60周年；其二，　1949年毕业于北京大学医学院的孙老，今年恰好也是从医、行医、传医60周年。

　　我们不禁为之感慨，孙衍庆老院长的行医之路与共和国一道，已然走过了60载春秋。

　　孙衍庆老院长的60年是杰出奉献、多姿多彩的60年；是救死扶伤，不懈追求的60年；是甘为人梯，桃李天下的60年；是功绩卓越，硕果累累的60年。为人"豁达宽容"，为学"笃志求新"，为医"赤诚济世"，为师"言传身教"，为官"一心为民"。在他的身上，体现了老一辈优秀医务工作者为祖国无私奉献、为人民恪尽职守、为患者满腔热忱的崇高精神。

　　我们怀着深深的敬意完成这本画册，藉此希望更多的人们了解孙衍庆老院长的辉煌历程，体味他的人生感悟，学习他的高尚精神。

　　60年燃情岁月。孙衍庆老院长的精神将永远激励安贞人为祖国的医疗卫生事业、为安贞医院更加灿烂的明天而努力奋斗！

　　在此，谨祝祖国繁荣富强，祝孙衍庆老院长平安健康！

## Epilogue

The year 2009 has special meanings for former President Sun Yanqing. Firstly, it is the 60th anniversary of the People's Republic of China. Secondly, it is also the 60th anniversary of his career as a doctor, which started with his graduation from the Medical College of Beijing University in 1949.

We are deeply impressed by the parallelism between his career and the course of the republic.

President Sun has spent the past six decades saving lives, teaching students, untiringly exploring his field, and making wonderful findings and outstanding contributions. As a person he is philosophical and generous; as a scholar he is bent on innovation; as a doctor he is sincere and virtuous; as a teacher he teaches by precept and example; as an official he is dedicated to the interests of the people. He embodies the older-generation medical workers' noble spirit of selfless service to the country, commitment to their duties, and heartfelt devotion to their patients.

We have completed this album with deep respect in the hope of making more people know the glorious career of President Sun, ruminate his reflections on life, and imbibe his noble spirit.

Former President Sun has spent the past six decades in passionate dedication. His spirit will eternally encourage the staff of Anzhen Hospital to strive for the improvement of health care in our country and a better future of Anzhen hospital.

We hereby wish our country prosperity and strength and our former President Sun Yanqing peace and health.